SPIRITUAL POWER OF TRUTH

Spiritual Power
of Truth

BY

JOEL S. GOLDSMITH

Author of THE INFINITE WAY

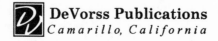
DeVorss Publications
Camarillo, California

ISBN: 087516-713-6
Library of Congress Control Number: 98-70583
Fourth Printing, 2004

DeVorss & Company, Publisher
P.O. Box 1389
Camarillo CA 93011-1389
www.devorss.com

Printed in the United States of America

CONTENTS

Ye shall know the truth,
and the truth shall make you free.

John 8:32

CHAPTER I

Invisible Selfhood

JESUS SAYS, "I can of my own self do nothing," and yet He went about healing the sick, raising the dead, feeding the hungry, and forgiving the sinner. Evidently, then, He was fulfilling that which He said, *"Thou seest me, thou seest the Father that sent me for I and the Father are One. The Father is greater than I, but I and the Father are One."* In other words, I, even as Jesus or even as Joel, am linked up with the invisible Selfhood so that the Selfhood of me is the Allness of me, and it is It which doeth the works. However, it is not an It out there, not an It up there; it is an It that is my very being.

Therefore to come into the completeness, into the fulfillment, of the Christ experience is to know the nature of God aright—to know that you are not dealing with a figure that you have to beg from, plead with, worship, and fear; not one that you have to be afraid of, that you have to sacrifice to or for. Know this Truth: that you are dealing with Life itself, always in expression. You are dealing with pure Life, a Life-being that is too pure to hold you responsible for even the sins of omission or commission.

Therefore release yourself from these complexes and realize that in the instant that you understand God as your true Being, you begin to purify your own consciousness so that the state of consciousness that enables you to do wrong no longer exists. In *that* there is the forgiveness, and only in that.

While we have the capacity to repeat our sins, we are in the position the Master spoke of when He said, *"Go and sin no more lest a worse thing come upon you."* He recognized that even though He lifted up the sinner to a certain extent, they still had the capacity to go and sin again. They had not completely received the Mind that was in Christ Jesus, and that was a task that each individual had to do themselves.

Any spiritual practitioner or teacher can forgive you your sins and release you from the penalty, but it only lasts a short time, because you still have the capacity to return to that same state of consciousness and to perform the same actions, or thoughts, or deeds. Dwell in this conscious realization of an indwelling Presence: "I can do all things through Christ"; "I can do all things through Christ which dwelleth in me. I can do all things through the indwelling Spirit."

If it so be the Spirit of God dwells in you, you are children of God. Therefore, in the consciousness of that Presence, constantly realized, you will find that a purification process goes on that dissolves the carnal mind with its belief in two powers, with its belief in two selves. Eventually, that mind that is in Christ Jesus is functioning as the greater part of your life, and the 10 to 20 percent remaining part of the carnal mind you can easily deal with as it tries to rear its head.

God, then, is not the source of any evil that afflicts you—past, present, or future; God is not the source of it.

You can in this very instant try it. Release God from all responsibility for any evil circumstance in your life—past, present, or future. Resolve within yourself that if you are ever tempted to believe that God is responsible in any way for any discord, you will reject it. If you are ever tempted to believe that God has visited or is visiting upon you any form of punishment, any form of sin, any form of disease, any form of discord, you will now absolve God from any responsibility.

Now, in this instant, make the change, and then after this you will merely have to reject the temptation whenever it returns to you. Release God from any blame, any responsibility, any censure that you may ever have had or felt. No evil that has ever come nigh my dwelling place has had its rise in God. God has never been responsible for any evil that has ever touched this world. God is too pure to behold iniquity. The fault does not lie in God. The fault, the responsibility, does not rest with God. God has not visited evil upon His children.

The story of Noah and the Ark is not the story of a God who saved out an individual and destroyed all the rest of the world. That story is the story of karmic law. In any age where a people, a nation, is living contrary to loving thy neighbor as thyself, they can eventually expect a flood, or a flood of bombs, or a flood of one nature or another that will wipe the evil right out of them, even if it has to take their human sense of life along with it; but do not place the responsibility on God.

If you can, then right now change all that and release God—loose Him and let Him go. "Never again will I fear God, never again will I look to God with any sense of responsibility for my ills. God is too pure to behold iniquity, and this I will maintain and sustain with every breath of my being. God is too pure to behold iniquity. God has

no awareness of whatever it is that is disturbing me. God
has no awareness of the evil in my mind or the disease in
my body or the lack in my pocketbook.''

Make this commitment a full and complete one. If you
cannot make it a full and complete one, go back into your
home and work towards this commitment until you have
actually set God free from all sense of responsibility, until
you are no longer in connection with any such belief. Then
all you have to do thereafter is watch as the temptation
presents itself to you to think of God in connection with
any of the evils of your world or anyone else's world—
and reject it instantly! Then you will be set free for the
next step. The next step will be the realization that the carnal mind, the belief in two powers, has produced this; but
now there is no belief in two powers on my part. I have
seen that two powers cannot be a part of the pure God.
There cannot be both good and evil in God.

Do you see what you have done? You have destroyed
the belief in good and evil in God. That is the religious
belief of the world, holding it in bondage to all of its
errors—the belief that there is good and evil emanating
from God; the belief that God creates both good and evil.

The Bible does say, "I [you] create good and evil." I
guess it means it, too. "I create it"; the human I, myself,
am creating the good and evil by whether I am entertaining the true God or whether I am merely accepting karmic law, and then praying to it to destroy itself. It cannot
do that, but we are released as we perceive the nature of
God as One. Just think of that: "Hear, O Israel, the Lord
our God, the Lord, is One!" That One is not a combination of good and evil.

It is your theological belief that holds you in bondage,
and here is the spiritual Truth that can set you free: "God
is One, God is Love!" This is not a combination of love

and hate, not a combination of good and evil, not a combination of reward and punishment. God is One! In Him there is no darkness at all. He is too pure to behold iniquity. In this, watch—*watch*—how you are setting yourself free, mentally and physically. You are entering a whole new consciousness of Life!

Of course, it is the function of our work to make it possible for us to attain not only some measure of that mind but also increasingly greater measures of spiritual awareness. It is for this reason that I give to you my own experiences for whatever benefit they may bring to you, for whatever help they may be to you in your experience.

Probably because I have never had a religious background of my own, I have not always known or understood the problems that some students have in attaining spiritual awareness. On one particular trip to London, I learned one of the great problems that students face, in perhaps a strange way. You know that an English bishop wrote a book in which he told the people of his church and nation that they must present a new image of God to the people. In other words, the people just are not attending church anymore, they are not being held by religion, and therefore, they must be given a new image of God and of prayer.

This book aroused a great deal of controversy. In fact, the book was called *The Debate*, and the biggest names in the Christian Church each wrote a chapter of this book giving their part of the debate, and nearly all agreed that the church must offer a new image of God to the world. However, they also all agreed that it must not be a true image—they must retain the major false image. It was in reading this book that I caught a tremendous flash of what it is that confronts many students and probably makes the Way so difficult.

We have all heard, of course, that Moses placed a veil on Truth and that Jesus Christ removed this veil. Well now, as I say, with my lack of a religious background I never knew what that veil was that was put on, and I never knew what the veil was that Jesus Christ took off. I certainly never believed that it was taken off for a very long period of time, because for the last seventeen hundred years, the Truth has been well veiled. However, until I read this book, I did not know the nature of the veil.

Then it became so clear that when it was given to our students in London, we really watched miracles take place in front of our eyes. There was a transformation in our entire work in England because the veil dropped away from me, too, when I saw the nature of what the veil had been—because that veil operates subconsciously, or unconsciously, as well as consciously. In fact, I am sure that the religious world, these very men who wrote those chapters, themselves did not know the nature of the veil that they themselves were recommending be kept on Truth.

Now in order to discover the nature of this veil, we have to go back to Moses and find out what *un*veiling he had that enabled him to put the veil back on. He could not have put a veil back on unless it had been off, and it was off in his consciousness. Well, if you remember his experience on the Mount, you will remember that God revealed Himself to Moses, and His name is *I. I am He, I Am!*

This is the unveiled Truth that enabled Moses to become a leader of his people, a liberator of his people, that enabled him to overcome Egypt without sword, without armies, without weapons, and deliver the Hebrew people, without clothing, without food, and yet fed and clothed.

This must have been the veil that he put back on—the hiding of the name and impersonal nature of God. Certainly we know that he refused to allow anyone but the high priest to know the name of God—because the knowing of that name sets anyone free.

Well, then, when we read that Jesus removed the veil, we see how true that was. He revealed, clearer than anyone has ever before done, that *I* is God. *I* is the bread of life, of your life; the meat and the wine. *I* is the resurrection, *I* is life eternal. *"I am come that ye might have life and that ye might have life more abundantly. I am the resurrection. I will never leave thee or forsake thee, I will be with thee unto the end of the world. Fear not, it is I. Be not afraid. Fear not, I am with thee. I!"*

Three hundred years later the veil is placed on it again and God is personalized. So it becomes not *I* am the Way, the Truth, and the Light, but *Jesus* is. You might as well make it Moses, or Elijah, or Bill Smith, as far as Truth is concerned; for the Truth is not that Jesus is the God-man, but *I* am. Not that Jesus is the Way, the Truth, and the Light, but *I* am; *I* in the midst of you! It is not a separate *I* up on this platform or a separate *I* two thousand years ago, but the only *I* there is: the *I* that exists when you say *I*, and not so much when you say it as when in the depth of your being you hear it.

Be still and know that I is God! It is not *I* two thousand years ago, it is *I* in the *midst* of *you*, the *I* that has never left you and that never will leave you. If you make your bed in hell, *I* will be with you. If you walk through the valley of the shadow of death, *I* will be with you. If you mount up to heaven, *I* will be with you. Therefore, when you perceive the nature of God as impersonal *I*, the universal Being, the veil is dropped from God and your eyes see God face to face; and you can give up all praying to God to do something for dear Mrs. Jones, or her child, and rejoice that you have discovered God, Omnipresence.

Do you see now the greater value of the word *Omni-presence*? Is there anything omnipresent other than *I*; *I* here, *I* there, *I* here and *I* there; *I* with the living, *I* with the dead, *I* with the yet unborn . . . *I!*

No one will enter the Kingdom of Heaven separate and apart from *I*. As you take that word sacredly and secretly into your consciousness, you will discover that there is a good reason for Scripture's saying, *"Be still and know that I am God."* Then let God be Omnipresence and Omniscience and Omnipotence. You will know why it says that *I* will never leave you. You will not be looking around for a man of two thousand years ago. You will understand that the man of two thousand years ago unveiled the Truth for you so that you would know that *I* in the midst of you am He, and that *I* in the midst of you is your bread, your meat, your wine, your water, your resurrection. That *I* is in the midst of you that you might have life and that you might have it more abundantly. Therefore you rest and you relax in that *I!*

Along this line, we have for many years said in our classwork that you will never know God aright as long as you have a concept of God in your mind, because you will be expecting something of that concept that you are entertaining, and it cannot fulfill. No concept of God that you can hold in your mind can fulfill your prayers. A concept is an image, a graven image, which you have made.

What difference does it make whether you use the word *God*, G-O-D, or whether you decide to turn it into M-I-N-D, or L-I-F-E, or S-O-U-L; are these not words in your mind? Are you not merely changing one word for another and then expecting the new word to do for you what the other word did not do? Sometimes you have probably even believed that you had to know each one of those words in its right order or God would not respond.

Over and over this has been made clear in this Message, and this is the most difficult part of the entire Infinite Way Message. Until you can overcome all the concepts of God you ever had and wash them right out of your mind—taking them up, one by one, whether they happen to be *Love* or *Life* or *Soul* or *Spirit*, until there is not a single word left that you can think of—you will not reach that place where you will experience God, because God is not a word; God is an experience.

So when you have realized that any word that you can use as a synonym for God represents just another concept, just another mental image—one that instead of being graven with a knife has been graven with your thoughts—once you have eliminated all that and have come to the realization that none of this is God, for only *I* in the midst of me is God, then you face probably the last hurdle: because the word *I* is no more God than the word *God* is God.

However, this is an easy hurdle to overcome, because *I* is my Self, and one thing you will agree with is that none of us know ourselves. Of that we can all be assured! None of us knows what makes us tick. None of us knows why we are, what we are, or how we got this way. All that we know about ourselves is that we are, that is all; but what made me this way, what made you that way, is unknown.

As a matter of fact, what way *am* I? I could ask a dozen people and get a dozen different answers! Whatever I think I am is only a mental concept of me, and a very biased one. I know that, because I know that what I think of different people is not the way they are, because I have heard other people speak of those same persons and it did not sound like the people I was thinking of.

So I know that the last hurdle is the easiest one.

You will never believe that a human being is God because you know enough about yourself to realize that that which you know as yourself cannot be God. So there is no danger that you will form an "I Am" movement and say, "I am God." You will not do that! You will know that when you speak the word *I*, you are speaking the most sacred and secret word that was ever given to man. It is one so holy that Moses realized that the people of his day would definitely misinterpret it; therefore he put the veil on.

The human being is not God. The human being is the man Paul spoke about, who is not even under the law of God. That man must die, and that man does die, in the moment that you realize *I* in the midst of me. This is because, first of all, it is a simple matter when you realize your own limitations—sins of omission or commission. You realize that these are not really you, and they are not *of* you. They are no part of you. You do not want them, and there is nobody trying any harder than you to get rid of them. Therefore you know they are not really a part of your identity. So you come to realize that the good you do is also not you; that sometimes, if it were left to you, you might not do it. You might not be quite so generous or loving or forgiving. Then you realize that something greater than yourself is performing this good, in you and through you.

Now here is where personal selfhood dies—first, as you commence to realize that the negative qualities that go to make up your humanhood—impatience, intolerance, bias, bigotry, prejudice—are not really you and are not even welcomed by you, so that your humanhood begins to die; then later, as you begin to realize that whatever of good qualities are flowing through you, these also are not so much you as the Real, the Divine of you, showing through. Then you have come to that place where you realize that neither the good nor the evil of human experience is of me. All that is me, is that which God is expressing as me, or through me, or in me. Then we have impersonalized the Self.

Remember, we have already impersonalized God by realizing God is the *I* of you and of me, God is the Selfhood of you and of me. Now we have come down to the actual experience of acknowledging that whatever there is of life, of Truth, of love that is flowing through me is really the Divine expressing Itself. In the same way, whatever talent or art or gift I may have is not of me; it is again the Divine expressing Itself in this individual way. No artist really made himself an artist. No inventor ever made himself an inventor. We have to be born that way, and actually it is a gift of God, each one in his own way showing forth some measure, some quality, of God.

In impersonalizing God, we realize God constitutes our being. Just think how differently we view each other the moment we stop seeing each other as male or female, rich or poor, good or bad and begin to impersonalize and witness the Divinity, that *I*. You cannot do it, of course, while mistaking the body for the person. You do it only as your attention is directed through the *I* and you realize that this individual is hidden and invisible—incorporeal, the spiritual *I*. I do not care what the human appearance is; I have seen it in prisons and I have seen it in hospitals; but it is still *I* back there, and all the rest of this is a masquerade!

The Truth, then—the unveiled Truth—is that God is incorporeal, the spiritual *I* in the midst of me and in the midst of you. This is unveiled Truth: God is incorporeal, the spiritual *I*, the *I* of every individual— the *I*, really, of the animal world and the vegetable world and the mineral world; the Consciousness. This is spiritual enlightenment, this is spiritual illumination.

Put the veil back on. Then God is God, or God is life, or God is Jesus. Now you have the veil back on: the moment you have personalized God or localized God, you have put the veil back on and you have taken yourself outside the Government of God. You are only under the Government of God when you relax in the realization "Thank you, Father; the Kingdom of God is within me, and *I* is Its name."

Relax and let this *I* function. You do not function It, you do not direct It, you do not wield It as a power. You relax and God functions, the *I* functions, as your meat, bread, wine, and water. The *I* functions that you might have life and have it abundantly. By this time you have become a listening ear. Your whole life is now lived as if all you were was a listening ear—because in that attitude and altitude of consciousness, this *I* lives in you, through you, *as* you. Or as Paul said, "*I* live, yet not I. Christ liveth my life." Or as Jesus said, *"Not I, the Father within."*

However, remember: the Father is not a male parent. The Father is *I*. My Father and your Father is the infinite *I* that I am, that you are—that *I* in the midst of you which, if you relax in It, will live through you, will live your life for you—generously, abundantly, lovingly, spiritually. Once you know this Truth, you can no longer take thought for your life—for what you shall eat, or for what you shall drink, or wherewithal you shall be clothed. You are then taking away the prerogative of God—the *I* in the midst of you that has come that you might have all this—if you take thought for your life. You do not live now by thought or by taking thought. You do not live by bread alone, but by every word that emanates from that *I* within you to which you have now become attuned.

As you become the listening ear, that still, small voice takes over. Remember, God is not in the whirlwind. God is not in your problems. God is in the still, small Voice that emanates from that *I* within you! We, as Joel, Bill, Mary, are a state of attentiveness, listening, alert always to the impartation that is to come from within. Therefore in the Infinite Way writings, you will read that you are never to say, "I am God," you are never even to think, "I am God," for this would almost be like trying to spiritualize your humanhood. However, you are to be alert to hear that still, small Voice utter Itself and say to you, "Be still and know that I, down here in the midst of you, Am God."

Watch that you do not allow that word *I* to be another word up in your mind, because this is dangerous. This becomes another image in thought, another concept of God, and it can do nothing for you. Now when you know that you are speaking about Selfhood, Being, then of course you cannot make mental images. You cannot make mental images of Self, of Being, of *I*. They have warned us in the Hebrew age, they have warned us in the Christian age, they have warned us in the Oriental age, not to make concepts of God, not to make images of God. However, we have thought that if we did not make statues of them externally, we could make a statue internally; but this we must not do!

Now, having impersonalized God and having realized why God is Omnipresence—because I am here and the place whereon I stand is holy ground—we must take the second step. While it is revealed in a few tiny places in the Master's Teaching, it is not explained; and it is, of course, *"Put up thy sword." "Thou, Pilate, couldst have no power over me." "What did hinder you?" "Pick up your bed and walk!"* This, in other words, is the nonpower of the appearance of evil—impersonalizing every appearance of evil.

This is difficult because we have a guilt complex about our own lacks or limitations. We have the feeling we should know better and we should be doing better, and therefore we tend to personalize evil in our own experience and think, "I am at fault." Humanly we sometimes seem to be. The only thing that can save us from that, again, is the word *I.* The moment we realize the meaning of the word *I,* we will see that it is impossible that *I* am responsible, and so we can impersonalize evil. We must be watchful that we do not personalize evil in our fellow man. It is in the impersonalizing of evil that healing work is brought about. It is not nearly as fruitful in the impersonalizing of God as in the impersonalizing of evil.

In other words, in the present state of our consciousness, when we can impersonalize evil, we do better healing work than if we merely impersonalized God. The reason is that behind us we have centuries of the belief that God is a great power over evil. Therefore all of our attention for centuries has been trying to get God to come into our experience to destroy evil. To begin with, there is no such God, and secondly, God does not do any such thing. This is a difficult habit of thought to break, this desiring of God to protect us from evil, or to take evil out of our lives. Evil is, in and of itself, neither a presence nor a power. Evil is nothing that God contends with, it is nothing that God overcomes or destroys.

The way we know this, beyond all doubt, is that as we come into this higher consciousness, this impersonalization of God, even for a momentary flash, all of the so-called evils begin to disappear, and later we realize that they never existed as entities or identities. Even where we have had evil people, we have witnessed them become friends and good people, and therefore we realized the evil was really in our concept of them, or the world's concept of them, and they were not evil people. The evil was not overcome—it was not there! Is it not said that beauty is in the eye of the beholder? Certainly we know that harmony, as in music, is in the ear of the hearer!

CHAPTER 2

"Before Abraham"

IMPERSONALIZE GOD and what do you have? You have divine Being, universally expressing Itself, universally manifesting Itself; before Abraham was, and unto the end of the world. This is what you get when you impersonalize God: you get infinite, divine Being, from the so-called beginning to the so-called ending. You also discover that there was no beginning, as there will be no ending, for life is a circle. It never began. It never ends. It Is! Before Abraham, It Is; unto the end of the world, It Is. It Is *I AM! I AM! Before Abraham was, I Am!* As one mystic said, "Before God was, *I am*"; and this is Truth. Before there was such a thing as a God concept in anyone's mind, *I am*. Someone else has said, "If there were not a God, man would have to make one."

Do you not see that this only promotes that we might live forever in darkness, that we have to make up a God, that we have to form a concept of God, that we have to have some image or idea, in our mind, of God? God is invisible, indescribable, incorporeal, infinite, from everlasting to everlasting, and who can draw a picture of that?

Who can invent a word to encompass that? The only word that has ever been shown forth that set men free is that word *I!* Whenever it was revealed, the veil was removed. Whenever God was personalized and finitized, or made an image in this or that religion, the veil was on again.

Why could the mystic see that God is closer than breathing, nearer than hands and feet, when there is nothing closer than breathing but I myself? We are to relax, to rest, in this consciousness, the creative Principle of life, the Reality of life, the Omnipresence, Omnipotence, and Omniscience that Is within me. Closer than breathing Is the Selfhood of me. Relax in It and let It perform Its work. This also shows you why it was said, *"He performeth that which is given me to do, He perfecteth that which concerneth me."* There is always this He, that is within me, that we identify as not a "He" but as an *I*, neither male nor female. This *I* unveils God, this *I* unveils the omnipresence of God in the midst of you, this *I* enables you to take the final step on the spiritual Path: the mystical step.

Take no thought! Let your prayers be without words or thoughts. Let your ultimate prayer be an absolute silence. Be still and know that *I* am come that you might have life—life more abundant. *I* in the midst of you will never leave you nor forsake you. *I* am thy bread, meat, wine, and water. *I* am the resurrection unto your body, and if you should destroy this body, in three days *I* in the midst of you will raise it up again. If you have lost body, mind, business, and home, *I* and only *I* can raise it up again.

Relax in that Truth, *I* in the midst of me is the only God, It knoweth my need before I do. It is His good pleasure to give me the Kingdom. I do not pray for it, beg for it, plead for it, tithe for it, or worship for it. I relax in It, that This in the midst of me may live my life abundantly. This that is my outer experience is the direct reflex action of the *I* that is my true identity.

Therefore, if I live in the awareness of this, inevitably my outer experience must show forth this inner Grace, for life is not meant to be lived by might or by power, by sweat or by tears, by striving or by struggling. Life is meant to be lived by Grace; but nobody attains a life by Grace until they know that *I* am God, *I* in the midst of me. Then relax in It and let *I* live as me—let *I* live my life. Then is life lived by Grace. It does not necessarily remove us from our business or professional or family life. It may, and sometimes does; but the infinite nature of God's Being means that there are infinite ways of God's Life being lived as our individual life.

You will see how it becomes easier and easier to live without the profusion of words and thoughts, except in the sense that we are receiving words and thoughts—not thinking them, but receiving them. They are being imparted to us from within our own being, and this really is the spiritual Way of life—living always under God's Grace, receiving the divine impartation that turns us always in the right direction. It does not overcome evil for us; it reveals the nonexistence, the nonpresence, of evil.

Scripture says that the evils will continue in the experience of those who do not dwell in this consciousness. You are going to find that this will no longer be true. As the divine Consciousness—the realization of this Christ, impersonalized, divine Consciousness—becomes the consciousness of mankind, there will be nobody living outside the Temple of God.

You can readily understand that it would be impossible for God to have one Will for one individual and another Will for another, or one Way for one individual and one way for another. Therefore when we pray "Thy will be done in me, Thy way be done in me," it is the spiritual Way we are talking about; not a special way for me, but Thy Way, which is meant for all mankind.

There has been, in all the countries we have visited, a tremendous falling off in church attendance, in all religions, and there has been a much wider reaching out for something other than what has been known. This is marked all over the world. More and more publishers are wanting Infinite Way writings, and publishers are wanting more of them in different languages. They are getting them because the demand is there for them.

This is only indicative of one thing: the mind of man is reaching out for something beyond his mind. Therefore there will only be one answer. We will not find God with our mind. God is not to be found with the mind; but when the mind is still, God in the midst of us reveals Himself and says, *"Be still, I in the midst of you am He and I am come that ye might have life, and that ye might have life more abundantly."*

Then you will know the meaning of the transcendental consciousness, the fourth-dimensional consciousness, that higher consciousness which, when It is ours, when we have attained It, lives the spiritual life and embraces in It all who touch our consciousness. Therefore be sure that there are enough periods in the day to be still, very still, and let the Spirit of God reveal Itself to you within, as It announces to you, *"I Am He!"*

I have been asked how the thought of good and evil came about in the Garden of Eden. My answer is: How do you know the thought of good and evil came about in the Garden of Eden? Have you experienced it? Why don't you wait a year and practice the lesson in these pages and then see whether the belief of good and evil ever does spring up. Now up to this minute, you have no knowledge that it did—none whatsover. So you are asking a suppositional question, and nobody could answer that. You will be able to answer it within a year. All you'll have to do is begin now to practice this lesson.

Think for a few minutes on the vital problems that are disturbing you. They can be your own, your children's, or your grandchildren's. As you think of them, ask yourself if these conditions are good or evil and who said so. Who told you that these conditions were good or evil? Remember, you are receiving instruction, and the instruction says that there is neither good nor evil. In spite of all the beliefs about it, you can't make it any more real than if you were to believe that two times two is five.

If someone were to give you two objects and then another two objects and then left the room, you couldn't get five objects out of them. It is an impossibility, regardless of what your belief would be, to get more than four out of two times two, or two objects plus two objects. This is because a belief can't make anything so. Now, all we want to know at this moment is: is this sin evil? Is this disease evil? The question that is also asked is: did God create it? Did God create evil?

I think you know better than that. If God created eternality or immortality—if there is nothing in God that defileth or maketh a lie—certainly God didn't create evil. If God didn't create evil, who did? Have you been entertaining a belief in good or evil? If you are, who gave you that belief? You don't know, but you will know a year from now. You will know exactly where it came from.

At this time, you can know nothing more than this: there is neither good nor evil. The entire first chapter of the Bible is dedicated to revealing a state of consciousness of spiritual perfection—wholeness, completeness—without material processes. It is dedicated to revealing that there is no other creation until someone accepts a belief in good and evil. Then what happens? The very moment that a belief in good and evil is accepted, we are outside the Kingdom of harmony, the Kingdom of God.

Then the moment we are outside, what happens? A material creation takes place. Now what created the second chapter of the Genesis creation? The belief in good and evil, and everything that is reported in the second chapter of Genesis as having been created, was created out of the belief in good and evil. It is not a God creation, it is not a spiritual creation. It is not subject to God and is not subject to the Law of God, nor is it subject to the Government of God. That is why spiritual healing cannot take place on a human plane.

Spiritual healing can only take place when you have stopped thinking of the person, and the condition, and the disease, and the belief, and the claim, and return to Eden where there is neither good nor evil, where there is only God, Spirit, wholeness and completeness. Nobody can ever be a spiritual healer who works from the standpoint of effect, who prays from the standpoint of trying to correct something in the Adam world.

If you succeeded in improving this picture, you would only have good materiality instead of bad materiality. You still would not be near the Kingdom of God. It is very much as I described previously, when I said that even on the human plane, you can be assured that within the next twenty-five years, all disease will be wiped off the earth. It will be wiped off by medical discovery. There will always be spiritual healings as long as there is disease left, but there will come a time when we will have no need of spiritual healers, for there will be no physical, mental, moral, or financial diseases to heal.

Certainly, the physical and mental diseases will, in the next twenty-five years or so, be entirely overcome by medical discovery. We might even say further that by that time, we'll have the thirty-hour week and everybody earning more than a thousand dollars a month. However, do you think for a moment that anybody is going to be happier than they are now? For heaven's sake, they are going to be more miserable! The saloons will keep open twice as many hours, and the televisions by that time will be having million-dollar prizes. Look how unhappy everybody is going to be who doesn't win them!

Don't believe for a minute that health and wealth are going to make you happy. I have never been among Truth students where there weren't some millionaires or very wealthy people. I have never been in a group where there weren't perfectly healthy people. Yet these people were Truth students. Why? They had not found happiness, they had not found peace, they had not found contentment, they had not found the center of their being. So never believe for a moment that attaining your physical health, or your physical wealth, is going to make you one bit happier than you are now. If anything, it is very apt to increase your unhappiness.

The answer to life is in coming back into the Garden of Eden, where there is neither health nor disease, where there is neither wealth nor poverty—where there is only a continuity of perfect joy and harmony, dependent on nothing. It is where there is just a state of IS, a state of Being, a state of God Being. We can return to the Garden of Eden at any moment. It will take a year of practice, but we can attain It.

Now, we do this in one way. Outwardly, you can't voice this to anyone without danger of being locked up. Outwardly, you have no right to say these things to anyone.

If you do, you take away from them their God. However, outwardly you can look on every form of evil and whisper, within yourself, there is no evil; only thinking makes it so. Nothing is good or bad; but thinking does make it so. Nothing is good or bad except when we place that concept on it. These are very strong words. The disciples were willing to leave the Master for far less strong words; but they are Truth.

You can only be in trouble as long as you entertain the belief of good and evil. Once you begin to look on all so-called evil conditions and say, as the Lord said to Adam, *"Who told you, you are naked?" "Who told you, you are evil? Who told you this is sin? Who told you this is disease? Who told you this is dangerous?"* you will see that God never said anything was evil. Did God ever say that to anyone? No. Please believe me, God never said anything was evil.

One time I was sitting in the presence of a person who was, to all sense, passing on. I was sitting there in the same discomfort that you would, realizing that I could do nothing to stop it. I had no miracle gifts to prevent it. I didn't know any miracle words that would turn it back. Something had to come to me from the depths of the Within or there was going to be a funeral. It didn't seem the right thing, so I could only turn within to that still, small Voice and wait and wait, and sometimes beg and plead for something to come.

Finally it came and these were the words: *This is my Beloved Son in whom I AM well pleased!* You wouldn't have believed it if you had seen him. No, you wouldn't have believed it. You would have seen evil, you would have seen disease in its last form. You would have seen a person's death; and then here the Voice says, *"This is my Beloved Son in whom I AM well pleased!"* I want you to know that it wasn't long until that became an actual fact in demonstration. Health, harmony, completeness were restored.

I had another occasion when I was called to my own father. He was also on his deathbed, so the hospital said. He was in an oxygen tent. I stood there in that same way: "I have no words of wisdom that are going to change that into health, I have no formulas, and I know no miracle-working words or potions." I stood there as you would do in front of your own father, but with this difference: I knew that if God uttered His Voice, the earth would melt. So I had to be still enough and receptive enough to listen and to hear. I finally did. Standing there, watching my father breathing through that apparatus, the words came, *"Man does not live by breath alone."* You know, it was far less than five minutes when he signaled for the nurse to come and take the instrument away. Two days later, he was out of the hospital.

Who said that was evil? God didn't say it; God merely said man shall not live by breath alone. Here is the belief in two powers—that we live by the breath; whereas we live by the Word of God. My father proved it—he lived by the Word of God, not by breath. Living by the word of God, if breath was normal and natural, it was there.

Let us be clear about this. The nature of error is purely an illusion. That was the great discovery of Gautama, the Buddha. As a matter of fact, he wasn't the Buddha, he was Gautama until that second when, sitting under the Bodhi Tree, the still, small Voice spoke to him. Do you recall why he was sitting there? He was looking for a remedy to sin, disease, death, and poverty. The Voice said, *"This is all an illusion."* From that moment, Gautama was Gautama, the Buddha or Enlightened One or Messiah or Christ.

The very moment that Gautama knew that there was no sin, disease, or death—that they were an illusion—in that moment he was the Enlightened One, the Messiah. The very moment that you perceive that there is neither good nor evil, then your function as a healer is not to remove or heal disease, or to believe that God heals disease, or that there are some formulas or affirmations that will remove disease. You will know the Truth that this whole mortal creation, whether it's healthy or sick, wealthy or poor, is all made up of the belief in good and evil. Now, in proportion as you overcome it, you know neither health nor disease, neither wealth nor poverty. You just know the Garden of Eden—a continuous outpouring of spiritual harmony.

You may never have an extra thousand dollars in the bank, but neither will you have a need for it. If you have, it will be there, because God appears in infinite form, at any given moment—but not unless you know the Truth, not unless you know that it is only the belief in good and evil that throws you out of the Garden of Eden. You will never be a spiritual healer while you believe there are two powers, the power of God and the power of sin or disease or lack or astrology or diet.

You will never be a spiritual healer until you know that we don't need any power. Nobody needs any power. God is maintaining His spiritual universe eternally and there is nothing wrong with it. There is something wrong with *us*. The belief in good and evil, in good powers and evil powers, in good conditions and evil conditions—these beliefs throw us into what we call the second chapter of Genesis, or material creation. There you find not God as the Creator but something that is called Lord God.

Lord, it is said, is synonymous with *Law*. In other words, you are under the law. That is the power you are under—law—when you are in the second chapter of Genesis. When you are in the first chapter of Genesis, you are under Grace. How can you get under Grace? Give up the belief in good and evil, and you find Grace permeates your entire being. Grace supports you, Grace heals you, Grace maintains you and sustains you. Grace is the power that goes before you to make the crooked places straight. Grace is all about you, and yet you have no more awareness of it than a fish has of water. The fish is swimming in it but doesn't know it. A bird knows nothing about air, but it's flying through it. You'll never find one, though, that will tell you so.

So it is with us: when we are in a state of spiritual health, we not only don't know disease, but we don't know health. We only know that we are harmonious, normal, free—and that's all we know. How can a healthy man describe health? He can't do it, because he doesn't know it. He only knows that he is in it, whatever it may be, and that it's nice to be in it.

Let us understand this. Let us begin, right now, to be spiritual healers. Let us understand that somewhere, somehow, sometime, we accepted a belief that is no part of us, and that belief is that there are two powers. That belief says that there is a God power that can do something for us—and there isn't. God power is already doing all that It can do. It is doing it in the Garden of Eden for all of the spiritual Creation—but it won't work in the second chapter of Genesis; it won't help you. That is why, as good and as moral and as benevolent as you may be (or your neighbors), you come under sin, under death, under accident, under wars. You ask how these things can be if there is a God. Well, there couldn't be if there were a God on the human scene. There is no God in the second chapter of Genesis; there is a Lord God, which is a law of cause and effect.

When you rise above the law of cause and effect, you are no longer under the law; you are under Grace. You will have to do this for yourself. Your practitioner can do it for you only to bring about a specific healing. You will have to do it yourself to come into a state of spiritual living in which you need no healing—in which, like the Master, Christ Jesus, you can heal all those who are un-illumined as to this Truth.

If you were to read the four Gospels with what you have learned here in mind, you would find the confirmation of it. You would find that although He never voiced it this way, He knew exactly this, and that is what made Him a spiritual healer and the Son of God.

He was able to say to Pilate, *"Thou couldst have no power over me unless it came from God."* He was able to also say, *"Put up thy sword, we don't live by material means. Man shall not live by bread alone. I don't need meat, I have meat the world knows nothing of. What did hinder you? Pick up your bed and walk! Neither do I condemn thee for the sins. Who did sin, this boy or his parents? Neither."*

Don't you see that all of this was the showing forth of His knowledge that there is neither good nor evil? He did not condemn evil, He didn't praise good, He didn't even *claim* good. There is no good except God. You must say that too. There is no good, there is no good health and there is no bad health, there's just God! There is no wealth nor lack of wealth, there's just God! There is no sin and there is no purity, there's just God! Just God; that's all there is: God. Now don't say that in that old absolute sense: "Oh, God is all." Don't say it unless you know that there is neither good nor evil.

When you know that, when you are convinced in your innermost heart that there is neither good nor evil, then you will know that all of this exists as a belief in the human mind, a belief that caused you to be thrown out of Eden. When the belief is overcome, you can say with the Master, "I have overcome the Adam world." "I have overcome this world, and I'm back in the Kingdom of Heaven, where there is neither good nor evil—there is just God!"

There is just spiritual being, just perfection: nobody knows what health is, because nobody knows what disease is; nobody knows what painlessness is, because nobody knows pain—there is nothing to compare with. Nobody knows what wealth is, because nobody lacks anything—therefore they can't know what lack is, and if they don't know what lack is, they can't know what abundance is. Don't you see that?

Please believe me. I have worked so many years in this Work. I have known from the beginning that we were dealing with a spiritual universe and that the evil in it wasn't real. However I never knew why, nor did I know how it came into this state of being out of Eden until a revelation came to me. The revelation came in those passages where God said, *"Who told you, you were naked?"* Then I knew that something was wrong. The knowledge of good and evil, Adam and Eve thrown out of Eden: that gave me the whole secret. Eden represents our spiritual domain. Eden represents a state of harmony, or Heaven. Eden represents our immortality, our state of Divine Being.

CHAPTER 3

Neither Good nor Evil

EDEN REPRESENTS our spiritual domain. Now what threw us out of that? What threw us out into what the Master called this world? It is just as plain as anyone can read. The knowledge of good and evil: that's what did it.

Now as we approach our healing work, we have no knowledge of good and evil. We have no knowledge of evil to be removed or risen above. Because so much of humanhood remains in us, we still recognize that we have before us the appearance of good and evil—the appearance of sin, disease, death, lack, and limitation. As long as we are faced with that, we can't be absolute and just say, "Oh, God is All; there is no error." You can't do that. You have to sit down and let God say it to you. *He uttereth His Voice and the earth melteth.*

When you hear the still, small Voice, or when you feel that Stirring within you, that divine Presence within you, you may be assured of this: whatever appearance of sin, disease, death, lack, or limitation is before you will melt away. Don't think for a minute that you can ever be so smart as to bring it about. Never believe that because you could go out of here and say, "Oh, there is neither good nor evil," it would work miracles in your life.

You must begin; and remember how Jesus said to pray: sacredly and silently. And I hope you are not going to be enough of a show-off to go out and tell this to anybody. If you do, you are only doing it to show off; you have no good motive. The only pure motive is to live spiritually and be a blessing to your fellow man, and you'll never do that by going out and telling this to anyone.

You have got to live with this for a year until you demonstrate it. You've got to live with this and prove it within yourself, until it becomes so self-evident that the world sees it in you. Now remember, if you are ever tempted to tell this to anyone, you are just trying to be a show-off, and you're going to lose what you got. You're going to lose the possibility of demonstrating it in this incarnation, because you can't trifle with the Word of God; you can't boast with it and play with it like a drama.

The Word of God is something sacred, something secret, and it should never be divulged—not for money, not for glory. Don't ever think that I am divulging this to you for the price of a class. You couldn't get this out of me for ten thousand dollars, nor a hundred thousand. Money won't buy it, and I can't gain name or fame by telling it to you. I am telling it to you out of the integrity of a spiritual life that is devoted to spiritual living and spiritual healing. I'm confiding in you my life's secret. It's not for you to go out and boast or brag about, or write books about. When the right time comes, I'll write books about it.

Right now, this must be lived, this must be demonstrated. You must have this as a Pearl of great price. If anybody wants it from you, let them prove they want it by giving up all they've got, by selling all they have, or else by earning their way to this teaching. You didn't buy your way in. There are loads of people who have more money than you have, and they are not in this teaching. You earned your way in by your consciousness. You earned your way to hearing this Truth. You're entitled to it, without money and without price. It's all yours.

However, remember this: I got it sacredly, and I've kept it sacred; and I have gone all around this world demonstrating it. The progress of the Infinite Way is the proof and the demonstration that this is Truth. So I can impart it to you from experience. You can only prove it in the degree that you hug it tightly within yourself. Keep it sacred; but use it. Use it morning, noon, and night with every bit of error with which you are confronted: in the newspaper, on the radio, in your family, on the streets.

Wherever you are confronted with error, turn within yourself and ask, "Can I be made to believe in good and evil?" "Can I be made to accept two powers? No, I won't accept good and evil." Then you won't be tempted to try and heal somebody or something. You'll just stay within yourself and know the Truth. There is only the Garden of Eden, which really exists, and we are in it, as long as we will not be made to accept appearances or judge by appearances—as long as we are willing to judge righteous judgment.

Righteous judgment says, "In the beginning, God created all that was made. God looked at what He made and found it very good!" That's Truth, and you shall know that Truth. Then as these ugly appearances stick up their heads, don't be fooled by them. Declare within yourself, "I can't be made to accept good or evil; I accept God alone as constituting the Garden of Eden." God is the very substance of man, the very substance of the trees, the very substance of the crops, the very substance of life.

God Is All in all, because there are not two. There is neither good nor evil; there is only Spirit, there is only Life!

I've been asked to speak of faith. Well now, I could tell you to have faith in what I just told you. However, I personally don't believe that is faith. I probably would say to believe in God, but I don't believe that is faith. Faith is something that God plants in us that is not faith but wisdom, knowledge. Let me rather say that I have faith that when you plant roses, you are going to get roses. I have faith that when you plant apples, you are going to get apples. I have faith that when you put two and two together, you are going to get four. Then you'll probably say that you don't have to have much faith about that—you know it. Well, that is what I think faith is: it's something that you know.

If you believe it without knowing it, that is blind faith, ignorant faith. Paul spoke about that when he spoke of the God whom you ignorantly worship. Everyone ignorantly worships God unless they know God. Just to believe in God because somebody said so, or to believe in God because it says so in a book—well, that's not knowledge; that's not faith. That is more or less superstition. That's why some churches have such terrible holds on some people. This is because people haven't any knowledge; they have ignorance and superstition, and that is easy to play on.

When people have knowledge, you can't hold them in ignorance, or superstition, or fear. That is what faith is— the knowledge of something. At this moment you might have blind faith or a measure of, shall we say, trust. What you have read here is Truth, but I really wouldn't care how much faith you had in it; it won't benefit you any until you have knowledge of it. And you will never have knowledge of it until you prove it by demonstration.

There is no way on earth that you are ever going to know that you have learned a lesson of Truth unless you demonstrate it, you prove it to be so. Brush all appearances aside and take your stand inwardly, peacefully, silently, and say, "I am not accepting good and evil. I am accepting the first chapter of Genesis, in which God created all, and all that God created Is good; and I'm standing on that Truth!" If you stand on it firmly enough without ever letting it cross your lips, then see harmony appear and have someone come up to you and say thank you for praying for them, or see the discord change right into a harmony in front of your eyes. When you've had *that* experience a few times, you can say, "Now I have faith, now I trust this Truth: I've seen it demonstrated."

Yes, there is an intuition which brings us a faith even before we see the signs—but even that is knowledge; and it isn't always necessary to see the signs to have knowledge. Many times we know things before we see the outward signs. That is another form of faith and is something that takes place in the life of every spiritual practitioner when they are doing healing work. There is no outward sign of any improvement—the pain is the same, the fever is just as high—and yet the practitioner inwardly says, "The healing has taken place." You may even say to the patient, "It's all right; you won't need me any more." There has been no outward demonstration or proof. But there is something which is equal to that.

There is an inner intuitive conviction which is a knowledge not based on appearances. It is a knowledge based on, shall we say, Christ, the Spirit of God that tells us the Truth—as It told me, "This is my beloved Son, in whom

I am well pleased." I had no evidence or proof; yet as far as I was concerned, that ended the treatment, that ended the case. The inner conviction was faith based on knowledge—but the knowledge wasn't based on sensory evidence; it was based on intuitive evidence. So we have faith in different forms and in different ways.

Sometimes students are a little bit afraid to declare that they haven't a faith or conviction for fear that it will be destructive to them. That is not good. It is much better to be totally honest and say, "I don't know . . . I don't know if there is a God." "I don't really know. I'm not disbelieving it, I'm not going to be an atheist. I am merely going to say, I don't know. I have no knowledge of it, no conviction of it. I can't go on this way, I must know, not just believe. I must know, and I must know positively." You know, when you are brave enough to take that stand, it won't be long until the Voice will utter Itself and say, "This IS Me, right here inside of you." Then after that, there will never be a question in your mind again. Even though you walk through the valley of the shadow of death, you won't doubt.

Now this thing of just believing because you are afraid to admit that you don't really know: that won't help you. That again is worshiping God ignorantly. Be totally honest. If you haven't had a God experience or a God conviction, acknowledge to yourself that you haven't, but that you want it, that you know it is a possibility because others have experienced it. It must come to you too, not to prove Itself, but because no man can live a happy life, a full life, until he has come to know God.

Up to that time, sensation can fill a part of your life, alcohol can fill a part, drugs can fill a part, vacations and trips to Europe can fill a part—but they can't make you happy, they can't make you content, they can't make you

at peace. Nothing is going to do that for you except the
experience that reveals God within yourself, the experience
that so reveals God within you that you can say, "It's all
right, Father, if I walk through the valley of the shadow
of death; it won't bother me." "Whether I live on this side
of the grave or the other side won't bother me, for now
I know that where I am, God Is—that where God Is, I am.
Now I know nothing matters, and I and the Father are
One. All that the father hath is mine, and the place whereon I stand Is holy ground! If I have no words, He will put
the words in my mouth. If I have no understanding, His
understanding is infinite. It makes no difference about me
now. I'm agreeing with Paul. I live, yet not I, but Christ
liveth my life. Christ fulfilleth me. I can do all things
through Christ. I can of my own self do nothing. The
Father within me, He doeth the works."

Now these things are not affirmations. They're not quo-
tations from the Bible. These are now living Truths, and
I can promise you this: everyone can have that experience
if they will dedicate themselves to this Truth, namely that
there is neither good nor evil. Refuse steadfastly to accept
appearances. Keep it secret, keep it silent, until It demon-
strates Itself. Don't lose it by spouting it. If you have
planted a seed in fertile soil, leave it there until fruit appears. Don't dig it up to show your neighbors. You'll
never get fruit.

The Master is clear that prayer must be secret, that
one's relationship with God must be secret and sacred.
Don't go telling it unless you have an intensly interested
student or class. If you have witnessed that they can sit
with you an hour, two hours, in silence, in stillness, and
still be interested and alert, still be alive, then you can bare
your heart to them. You can share everything that God
has given you with such people. But don't do it with any-

one else, because they will trample on your Pearls. The Master told you that this world will trample on your Pearls—they'll take them right out of your hand and sell them at the five-and-dime store for junk. That is how worthless they will make your Pearls appear if you let them.

Keep these things sacred. Don't even tell them to your nearest relative unless that nearest relative is as willing to pay the price as you are—the price of study, the price of meditation, the price of devotion. Do you see that? Then you can share, and share liberally. Then you can go up and down the world and preach the Gospel. Then you will find that the world will beat a pathway to your door to find it.

The Master told His disciples when He left this scene that they should preach the Gospel and go out and heal the sick. He told them to let this Truth be known, but to be sure—very sure—that those they instructed were "those of your household." He told them to be sure that they are those who want not just the loaves and fishes, but this inner secret to live by.

The principle of this message—or let me say, one of the unique principles of this message—concerns the word *impersonal*, or *impersonalization*. Since this is a unique principle, since this is one that is not ordinarily found in religious teachings, it becomes necessary to understand it thoroughly and to learn how to apply it in the experiences of daily living.

I will start with an illustration. Heretofore as humans we have looked first to parents for our good, then later to employers or brothers or sisters or friends. For one thing we look to parents, for something else we look to children, and for something else we look to brothers or sisters or friends. It is a part of natural, normal, human living to look outside ourselves and to look to others for those things which actually we already have embodied within our own being.

The reason we do not know this is that we have thought of ourselves as being limited to our education or environment, or limited to our finances. We have so thought of ourselves in this way that we have brought forth the demonstration of limitation. Whereas, if we knew that I and the Father are One and that the Father has said, *"Son, thou art ever with Me and all that I have is thine,"* or if we were to consciously remember that I and the Father are One, not two, and that all that the Father hath is embodied within us as the Son of God, we would then know that what we call our self is not to be spelled with a small s but with a capital S.

In other words, this which we call Joel would merely be the outward form of my self, but my Self is that Divine Son of God which is One with the Father, to which has been given the God-given dominion over all that is, and to which the Father has given His own Allness. Now once we begin to realize that our self is not a personal, limited self, is not a self limited to our personal sense of good, we should realize that our Selfhood, our real being, is God; or that which we call Joel is but the outer form of individual expression. Therefore, Joel is not limited to Joel; Joel has access to his Self. Therefore when we meditate, when we make contact, we make contact with our Self, our Divine Self, our real Self, our Infinite Self. From the moment that we have contact with It, Infinity begins to flow forth—Immortality, Eternality.

Let us think for a moment of a seed, the seed that you are going to plant in your garden—a rose seed, an apple seed, any seed. As you look at that seed, you must agree that it is limited. It is limited to its seed self. Now what can a seed do or become? The answer is nothing. A seed by itself will always remain a seed. It will never be more than just a seed. It can become less: it can wither and die and be even less than a seed; but more than a seed it never can be of itself.

Now, planted in the earth, let the seed be one with its source. Give it access to all that surrounds it, to all that is its real life and being. Then your seed evolves and becomes the rosebush with dozens of roses, or the apple tree with hundreds upon hundreds of apples, all from a seed that of itself was nothing.

The Master says, *"I, of mine own self, can do nothing." "If I speak of myself, I bear witness to a lie. I and My Father are one, and I can do all things that the Father doeth. I can be all things that the Father is. I am the life, I am the Truth, I am the Way, I am the bread, and wine, and water."* Remember: He said that I can of my own self do nothing, but through My God Self, through my God Being, I can do and be all things. So it is, then, that as the seed is restored to its native element in the soil, all that is in the soil begins to pour forth through the seed and eventually becomes the full-blown product. So with this "I" which of myself is nothing: the moment I go within to my native soil, which is my inner Selfhood, my inner Divine Being, and become One with the Vine, I can then bear fruit richly.

Everything from the Godhead can now pour forth through me and I am no longer limited. I am no longer limited to my age or to my bankbook or to my education, because now I am drawing up from the depths of my inner Being all that is necessary for my experience. Now because of our false education, we have accepted Joel as my self and have learned never to look within but rather to look out there, to put faith in princes or to put hope in man whose breath is in his nostrils, or in political preference, influence, birth, and so forth. However with the revelation of my true Being, my true Identity, I realize that the Self of me is God. Therefore, I can reach down into this Withinness and find myself One with the Vine, One with the Christ, One with my Divine Sonship, One with my Divine Selfhood.

The moment that contact is established, it is exactly as if a Voice said, *"I am with you. I am going before you. I will become your bread, your meat, your wine. I will appear outwardly as your opportunity, as your companionship, as your home, as your safety, as your security. I will do all things for you."*

The moment I have made that contact with that Divine Self, I no longer look to parents or to children or to neighbors or to friends or to brothers or to sisters. I look within my Self, make contact, and then I'm patient until the flow begins to come from within to the without. Then I find that I do not have to depend on those outside of me but rather I can share of this infinite Storehouse with them until they, in their turn, learn the infinite nature of their own Being and begin to draw on it.

In other words, when the Master says, *"If I go not away, the comforter will not come to you,"* He is indicating that we may draw on Him until such time as we too have gained the realization that He before us has gained. *"I, in the midst of thee,"* the *I* in the midst of thee, is your wine, your water, your bread—the Presence that appears in your experience as Divine harmony.

Turn each day in one of your periods of meditation to the realization that God within me Is the Self of me. "God is my true Selfhood, my Infinite Selfhood, and it is my Father's good pleasure to give me the Kingdom. My Father knoweth what things I have need of even before

I speak. Therefore in this meditation I need only acknowledge, Father, that Thou art closer to me than breathing, in the very midst of me; and because Thou art the Infinite Intelligence of this universe, Thou knowest my need even before I do, even before I could possibly ask. It is Thy good pleasure to give me the Kingdom, whatever that may be. It is Thy good pleasure to forgive me my sins. It is Thy good pleasure to go before me to make the crooked places straight. It is Thy good pleasure to be my constant companion. It is Thy good pleasure to be my bread, my meat, my wine. Thou art my bread, my meat, my wine. Thou art my life eternal. Thou art my resurrection. Thou, Father, in the midst of me, art my Infinite Supply, my eternal life; and only from the Divine Fountain in the midst of me will I look for my good to flow.'' You see, in doing this you are now dying daily to the belief that someone external to you owes you something; that someone external to you must provide for you; that you are dependent on a person, a group, an employment, an investment; that you are in any wise dependent except upon this Infinite Self which is your Being.

It becomes easier for you when you think of yourself in terms of capital S instead of small s. Think of yourself as being the Son of God, think of yourself always with a capital S, as one with God, heir of God, joint heir to all the heavenly riches. Then you will find that you have impersonalized yourself, because gradually you will come to realize that you are not finite being, you are not man, whose breath is in his nostrils, you are not that creature who is not under the Law of God—neither indeed can be, for you now consciously have the Spirit of God dwelling in you; and according to Scripture, this makes you the Son of God, the Child of God. *If so be the Spirit of God dwelleth in you, then are you the Child of God*—the Spirit, the consciousness.

If it so be that the consciousness of the Presence of God is in you, then you do become the Child of God, no longer mortal, no longer material, no longer finite, no longer dependent on any circumstance or condition external to your own Being, dependent now only on your conscious union with God, your conscious Oneness. By virtue of this Self, you are now bringing forth your good into expression, or are permitting it to flow into expression.

Think of what this means when we come to seeing other people. Remember, now, that what we have declared of ourselves is also true of them. What I have just declared to be true of Joel, you have now been declaring true for yourself—because if it is true of Joel, it must be true of you; for God is no respecter of persons. God is not a superhuman being that deals in personalities, liking one of us and not liking another. God is too pure to behold iniquity. God sees us as His own image and likeness, and therefore anything that is true of Joel must be true of you. Therefore God is your Selfhood, and your Selfhood is infinite; and it is from your Selfhood that the flow of good begins to appear.

Now this is established in you, and you meditate upon this. You practice this day in and day out in your meditations until—and it will not be too long—you will begin to see this fruitage appear. Remember, you are to bear fruit richly and you are not to deceive yourself or hide from expecting rich fruitage; rather you are to consciously remember that because of your identification with God, your Father, the Father within you, your real Self, you can now expect that rich fruitage to appear.

Once this has been established in you, you have another

function. You have to begin secretly, silently, and very sacredly to look around at the members of your household, the members of your family, your friends, and remember what you thought they were and begin now to change your concepts of them so that you realize that all that you have been declaring for yourself, all that you are now knowing to be the Truth of yourself, is likewise true of them. They too are One with this Divine Selfhood.

The fact that, for the moment, they do not know it, is none of your business. We are not dealing with *their* demonstration but *your* demonstration; and you will not have a demonstration unless you begin to perceive that this Truth that you have declared and realized about yourself must be a universal Truth. Therefore regardless of their lack of demonstration, regardless of their lack of willingness to even learn about their true Identity, you are secretly and silently knowing It.

Know this at your employer's business or among your employees or with your customers or clients. You are knowing this, in the classroom, of both teacher and pupils. You are knowing this in the government. It makes no difference what these people may seem to be or be doing: you are now realizing their true Identity. You are now realizing their Oneness with their Source—the universal Source!

CHAPTER 4

Your True Identity

W HEN YOU are realizing someone's true Identity, you are realizing their Oneness with their Source, and this is the reason not to give them a treatment. Save yourself from being a malpractitioner, because unless you are seeing them as they really are, you are malpracticing them, and your malpractice comes home to roost.

You know that our malpractice of other people never harms them, and their malpractice of us never harms us. Malpractice acts as a boomerang. It goes out from us and eventually hits nothing because it's only aimed at our *concept* of somebody, not at that somebody. It therefore turns around and returns to us and cuts our head off. In one way or another, malpractice is a boomerang. It never strikes those at whom it's aimed. It always turns around and reaches the sender.

Not all malpractice is malicious. Not all malpractice is intended to harm anyone. But unless you are seeing everybody, even your enemies—and this is the meaning of prayer—as One with God, joint Heir; unless you are seeing that Self with a capital S as the true Identity of everyone; you are malpracticing. You are sort of setting up a new hierarchy. For example, "I and my friends are all perfect, and only the rest of the people aren't." This isn't true.

The Truth is we are all One in Christ Jesus. We are all offspring of God. We none of us have human fathers. We have but one Father. The relationship of the human father has no relationship to the word *Father* at all. There is but one Father in this universe, and that is God. All the rest of us are offspring of that One Divine principle, and we are malpracticing when we do not recognize this Truth.

Now we have impersonalized our sense of self as applied to myself. We have now impersonalized our sense of self as applied to yourself. We have impersonalized our sense of self as applied to all of the people of this world, including our enemies. Just imagine what happens when you sufficiently meditate on this Truth so that you do not recognize any selfhood apart from God. Could you possibly suffer loss or destruction from another if there is no other than God? Can you ever be the victim of injustice, inequality, or any other evil if there is no selfhood other than God?

This applies very much to our work where we have cases at law. It is a very frequent occurrence, in our practice, that when students, patients, and friends are brought into court or are caused to be in court in some kind of a case, the biggest word there is *justice*, because nobody is in court for any other purpose than that of securing justice. Therefore unless you are seeing God as the Selfhood of yourself, of judge, of jury, of attorneys, of solicitors, of prosecutors—unless you are seeing the Self of all—how can you possibly expect justice?

Can you expect justice, equity, and mercy from man, whose breath is in his nostrils? If you do look for it there, you are apt to come out very disappointed in all of your relationships in life. Unless you are looking for your good—for justice, for equality, for mercy, for understanding, for cooperation—in the Divine Self of all being, of every individual, you are looking amiss and you may not find it.

So it is, then, that your concentrated meditation on this subject will eventually bring you to the conscious awareness, the actual conviction, that God constitutes the Selfhood of every individual. Therefore Self must be spelt with a capital "S." So if you are going to court, or if you are going to an employer, or to the union for justice, be sure that you are expecting it from the Divine Selfhood of individual being. Be sure that you are recognizing God as that Selfhood. Then you will have impersonalized it.

This is likewise true in our healing work. The first step in our healing work is impersonalization, and you must understand this. It is a contradiction of all metaphysical practices, however. The Infinite Way in its healing work is directly opposite to all other metaphysical teachings, for the following reason: we do not look within you for the error that is causing your trouble. We do not look to your wrong thinking for the cause. We do not look to the sins for the cause. We do not admit that resentment, jealousy, malice, sensuality, or any of these are causes for your ills. We do not agree that the cause of your illness, or your poverty, or your sin lies within yourself.

We start with the Self with a capital S which impersonalizes you and makes God your Selfhood. Therefore Divine qualities are the only qualities of your being. Therefore there is no sin in you, nor is there any effect of sin in you, nor is there any disease in you, nor is there any cause of disease in you. Rather, all evil which seems to be manifesting through you is recognized as impersonal—

as being no part of you, since God is your being. Even your body is the Temple of God; therefore this evil can not be in you or in your soul or in your mind or in your being or in your body. Where is it then?

Where is this evil? It is in an impersonal belief in mortality, in mortal selfhoood, in a sense of separateness from God (which you aren't). You aren't separate from God; you are One with God. Therefore we can give the commonly known names of *devil* or *carnal mind* or *mortal mind* to this impersonal source of evil, and the moment we have done that we have separated it from you.

The moment we believe that your wrong thinking, or your wrong doing, or your wrong mother or father are responsible for your ills, we have personalized the whole thing—placed it in you and made it virtually impossible to get it out. Whereas if in our healing work we recognize that God constitutes your being and therefore this evil, regardless of its name or nature, is but this impersonal carnal mind, this universal belief in two powers, this universal belief in a selfhood apart from God, then we have impersonalized it. We have, in more than half the cases, brought about this healing, and the other half we will bring about if only we will stick to this principle faithfully and persistently until we have overcome the belief within ourselves that there is anyone separate and apart from God.

See what happens the very moment that you have a grievance against anyone. You have the belief of injustice from them, or lack of money, or lack of cooperation, and you are pinning the evil onto them, or into them, that we have just removed from you. In other words, your demonstration consists of the ability to impersonalize, and that means that regardless of who it may be that you think is ungrateful to you, unjust to you, immoral to you, neglectful of you, you must reverse this instantly and realize that you have been guilty of malpractice. You have been guilty of seeing God's child as if he were a sinner, God's child as if he were ungrateful, unlawful, unmerciful. You must begin to realize God as the Selfhood of individual being, thereby impersonalizing.

There is a wonderful experience of impersonalization in Scripture in the story of Sapphira and her husband, where, after the crucifixion, the disciples had banded together but, because of persecution, had gone underground. They could not tend to their fishing, they could not tend to their ways of earning a livelihood. While they were being persecuted, they agreed to put together in one fund all that they owned so that all might be supported out of this common fund until the period of persecution passed.

The story goes on that they did put all that they had into this common fund in the care of Peter. However, Sapphira and her husband decided to hold out a little. Peter discerned this and he said to them, "You have not done this unto us, you have done this unto God." In other words, there is no us but God Selfhood, and so it is unto God that they had done this. We are told that both Sapphira and her husband dropped dead. In the very moment they consciously wronged God, the evil winged back on them and destroyed them. God didn't do it.

The evil that they aimed at this band of disciples really came up against the Selfhood of God, which is invisible and incorporeal. There was nothing there and nobody there to receive it, and it had to boomerang right back on the sender. So the evil that was destined against man was directed to its rightful source, God, and because there was nothing there to aim evil at, or hit, it boomeranged and destroyed the sender.

Now, we have two things to remember. One is that it wasn't really Sapphira or her husband that held out. Really and truly, it was this carnal mind operating through them; and since this carnal mind isn't a person and hasn't a person in whom and through or upon whom to operate, it becomes nothingness when you impersonalize it.

Now, begin to agree that you have not done this unto me, because there is no me separate and apart from God. I have no selfhood except for the capital S Selfhood; therefore you have not aimed this at me but at God. You will find that you have impersonalized your Self, and any human error that is aimed at you will not strike you. Then remember that those who aim evil in your direction are really not aiming it at all; they are merely instruments through which the carnal mind is operating. You will thereby more than likely release them from their sin and bring about their forgiveness.

In other words, if you personalize it and say, "You have done this unto me," it may turn around and strike back. If it did, it would be the fault of the sender in the sense of allowing themselves to be used. However, we want to go higher than being avenged. We want to go higher than seeking revenge upon someone. We want to see those who do evil to us forgiven, released from whatever evil is grasping them.

So the safe way is, if in your experience there is any ingratitude aimed at you or any lack of mercy or injustice, realize, first of all, your capital S Self and then realize "This is really not aimed at me at all, this is aimed at God." Also realize that it isn't even people or a person who is aiming it; they are merely the innocent victims, ignorant victims, of the carnal mind—of the ignorance shown in "Father, forgive them, they know not what they do." You will have nullified this carnal mind, since it is devoid of persons, in whom, on whom, or at whom to operate, and you'll find how quickly you will come into your freedom—a joyous freedom.

You are free when you're living in a world where no one has anything against you. If there does seem to be anyone, you've now recognized that it isn't personal—it's an impersonal source which is really not a power. You must see that this act of impersonalization is a conscious one. It will eventually explain to you why you could sit around from now until doomsday praying to God for something and it wouldn't come; or you could sit around from now to the end of time praying for justice or cooperation or gratitude, and not get it. In other words, good can only come into your experience through an act of your own consciousness. There is no outside God to see that you get mercy, or justice, or kindness.

Every week a group of the most wonderful, unselfish individuals bring about the release of some man from prison, or a woman, who has been sentenced either to life imprisonment or to death, who at the time of their sentence was innocent of the crime. They manage to find not fewer than fifty-two of these people in prison every year —and don't you know that they and their relatives were all praying for justice when the sentence was passed for life imprisonment or the death penalty, though they were innocent of the crime. You ask, what good were their prayers? The answer is *none*—because that type of praying is not prayer, it is ignorance.

Do you want justice, equality, mercy, and kindness from this world? Then begin in your meditations to impersonalize the evils of this world and begin to know that you are not the source of evil to anyone. This is because God constitutes the Selfhood of your being, and no one else is the avenue or channel of evil towards you, for God constitutes their Selfhood. Any evil apparent in your world is a product of a universal thing called the carnal mind, or mortal mind, which in and of itself is nothing until you give it a person in whom, on whom, or through whom to operate.

You see, the responsibility is upon your shoulders, because the Master says, *"Ye shall know the Truth and the Truth shall make you free"*; but He doesn't say the Truth will make you free without your knowing the Truth. All harmony and success in life is up to the individual, and to sow to the Spirit means to impersonalize to the extent that you realize God as the true identity of every human, every animal, every plant.

Once you begin to perceive that there is only one Life and that God is the Life of the human, of the animal, of the vegetable, and of the mineral, you will find all life flowing joyously to you. That is also the only way where eventually it comes about that the lamb and the lion lie down together. Once it is perceived that the Life, the Mind, the Soul of the lion is the Life and the Soul and the Spirit of the lamb—for they are one—then with your recognition of this, it will come about.

I have witnessed this dozens of times—not with lions and lambs, I must admit, but with cats and dogs who are always chasing birds. It seems to be their nature to chase birds and kill them, sometimes for food and sometimes just for wanton destruction. However, there have been dozens of times over the years when I have been called into homes where there were cats and dogs of that nature, and with just a treatment I completely dissolved that bestial nature of the cat and dog. It made it possible for them to be friends with birds, just through the realization that there's only one Life, there's only one Soul in this universe.

There is only one Being in this universe. God is the Life of all of us, and the Life of God doesn't end with a human being. The Life of God is infinite; therefore the Life of God is the Life of you, and of me, and of the animals, vegetables, and minerals. God constitutes the Life of all that lives and breathes; even the rocks and the stones are living things. They are not inanimate, as they appear to be. They are living things and they breathe, and God is the Breath of their being. This too, you see, is impersonalizing. It is really making God the Divine Self, the Self of you and of me and of her and him and it.

As we meditate on this, day in and day out, its Truth begins to unfold from within ourselves, and we gain the conviction of it. I can give to most of you, I might say to all of you, this letter of Truth, and to some of you convey even the very spirit or consciousness of it; but for most of you, it will be necessary to meditate.

Ponder this until something wells up within you and says, "This really is true, this is the Truth of Being. God does constitute my Selfhood, and therefore my Selfhood is not subject to weather or climate or hate or envy or jealousy or wrong thinking. My Selfhood is intact in God. My Selfhood is intact in its immortality. It is not subject to the beliefs of mankind, it is not subject to the beliefs of mortality. My Selfhood does not age, my Selfhood does not change. My Selfhood is Divine, Immortal Being— God!"

Yes, let's be awfully quick the very moment we catch the realization that this is true about us, and let us immediately turn to every member of our household and then widen that circle until we have taken in the entire world. It is realized that God constitutes individual Being; then you will see that there is no selfhood but God. For this reason, then, we do not pin error onto any individual—not even ourselves. We do not claim that our jealousy, our envy, our greed, our lust is responsible for our ills—because we haven't any such qualities. Any such qualities that may be temporarily expressing themselves through us must be recognized as having their source in the impersonal, carnal, or mortal mind.

Not only is this principle of impersonalization one of the most important in our work, but you must work doubly hard to embody it in your consciousness because you will not find it except in this literature. You will not find it in your experience until you make it your own.

You will see why we do not use the name of the patient in our treatments. You will see why we never say "you" in a treament, or "he" or "she" or "it." You will see why we never say to a patient, "You must be more loving" or "You must be more generous" or "You must be more patient." Why? We merely present the Principles of Being, and so, when giving a treatment, how can I treat you for something when I know there is no you except the God Self which is you?

Our work is to free ourselves from universal claims. I know that you do understand this, but I give it to you because you will have an occasion, every single day of your life, to remember what I am saying to you. The temptation, in our work, is to try to improve the human scene: we see a sick person and our first normal reaction is to want to see them well. We see an unemployed person and the very first thought is how we can bring about employment. We see a poor person and the first thing that comes to us is how to bring supply to them. We see an unhappy person and our first thought is how to bring happiness to them. Now if we persist in that, we will fail in our ministry.

It is for this reason that even though you perceive what

I am saying to you now, you will be under the same temptation tomorrow to violate it, and the same the next day, and you will never outgrow it. Never, unto the end of your days on earth, will you overcome the automatic, unconscious temptation, at least once in a while while giving treatment, to change the appearance into its opposite.

Now, that is natural to you, and it is natural to me. That was natural, undoubtedly, to Jesus Christ or He would not have had to go away forty days to the mountaintop to renew Himself. He would not have had to go away from His disciples every once in a while to renew Himself—because the only renewal that we ever need is to break the mesmerism of appearances. That is the only reason we ever have to pray. That is the only reason we have to commune. That is the only reason we ever have to go away to be still. There is no other reason.

We are already beyond the temptation of stealing. We are already beyond the temptation of committing adultery. We are already beyond the temptation of lying, or cheating, or defrauding. So we don't have to go away to the mountaintop to pray about those things. However, while we are not mesmerized by those forms of error, we are still mesmerized to some degree with good manhood. We are not easily tempted into the bad side of humanhood, but we are easily tempted toward the *good* side of humanhood. Of course, the good side of humanhood is only the opposite of the bad side, and in the end it can be just as bad as the bad side.

So it is that first of all, when we sit down to help ourselves or others, our realization—or one of our realizations—must be "I am not trying to change sick matter into healthy matter. I am not trying to change a little matter into a lot of matter. I am not trying to make unhappy people happy. My aim in this meditation is to realize, behold, and demonstrate the Christ''—in other words, demonstrate the Christhood of your being, of my being, of his being, of her being. That is why we are never trying to get something or get rid of something. We are never attempting to draw something to us or force something away from us. Our entire ministry is Christ Realization.

Now you, in your true identity—and this means *he, she,* or *it,* and the true identity of all—are the Christ, the offspring of God. There's nothing that you or I can do to *make* it so; it already is so. God already Is the life of individual being. God already Is the soul and the spirit and the mind. God already Is the integrity of every individual. That was established in the beginning before Abraham was. However, it is not manifest, visible, until One with God is a majority, until one individual can sit in silence and realize the Christ, spiritual Identity, true Identity.

Of course, the Christ will never take form in your mind; you won't see perfect man. You will only realize, or understand, or feel Christ. Christ isn't visible to the eyes, audible to the ears. Christ can't be touched with the fingers or smelled or tasted. Christ is really what you and I are incorporeally: a state of Divine Consciousness. That is what we are. But that is not what we appear to be to each other.

Looking out through the eyes, we behold a finite concept, a limited concept, a material concept of that which actually is. The only way that I can describe this to you is to tell you that if you were to show me one of those one-hundred-thousand-dollar masterpieces of painting that are sold so often, it would mean nothing more to me than some colored paint on canvas. I probably wouldn't give you ten dollars for it, so far as value to me is concerned. It wouldn't represent more than that to me, because I have no awareness of what you would call valuable paintings.

It's entirely different if you were to show me bronze, ivory, wood, or tapestry. There the situation would be different. I might see a thousand dollars in something that another person might not see ten dollars in, because I do perceive the nature of those other things that I don't in paintings. In the same way, without music appreciation you might hear the most glorious piece of music in all the world and beg somebody to turn it off because it breaks your ears.

So it is with this. We look out with our eyesight, which means with our limited, finite senses, and we are looking at God's masterpiece, *you.* That's God's masterpiece, His own offspring of His own Being, His own Self made individually manifest. Now, beholding it without spiritual appreciation, comprehension, we say, "Isn't this worthless!" Do you see that?

Now with your eyes closed to all appearances, realize that it makes no difference who has called you for help. It could be someone with the deepest sin, for all we know, or someone in a physical distortion beyond description. Now with eyes closed, remember, "Father, I'm not trying to change this picture. Give me Thy Grace to behold him as he Is. Awaken me out of this mesmeric dream so that I do not judge by appearances. Let me see him as he Is, and I will be satisfied with this likeness. Here, indeed, Is the Christ of God, the very spiritual offspring of Divinity. Grant me Thy Grace that I may see him as he Is, that I may see this situation as it Is. Reveal Christ where there seems to be a human being."

Then, as you sit in that silence, waiting, the Spirit of God touches you and illumines you, inspires you; and for a brief, fleeting second it is almost as if you could see, or touch, Reality—sometimes even smell It. For sometimes in this deep meditation of Realization the whole room is filled with the perfume of flowers. There may not be a flower within a mile of you, but the entire room is bathed in a perfume of flowers. The Spirit of God may also come as music that has no earthly tongues. It makes no difference how It comes. It may come as a light, or It may come as a deep breath.

Whichever way It comes, if you have been clear that what you are seeking is not changing a human being from bad to good, or poor to rich, or unemployed to employed, or sick to well, but rather beholding Divinity instead of humanhood, then sooner or later, the experience will come to you. It may only be momentary; but in that momentary flash, your patient will be improved, benefited, healed, employed, enriched—whatever the situation demands.

Certainly there are those instances where the fullness of the healing does not appear in that one realization, no matter how deep it may be, and you may be called upon to do it twice, or ten or a hundred times. It's because the opacity may lie with your patient or student, in that, before they can experience the harmony, there must be a change of consciousness, which is to be outwardly pictured as the harmony. Always remember that we are not healers of the body; we do not change the body at all. Our work changes the consciousness of an individual, and the changed consciousness appears outwardly as harmony, as health, as supply, as companionship—whatever the need may be.

CHAPTER 5

Universal Hypnotism

WE ARE not healers of the body. Our work does not change the body at all. Our work changes the consciousness of an individual. One of the great stumbling blocks is that most people have a definite idea of what it is they're seeking when they ask for help, and of course that may not fit at all in the spiritual picture.

I have told of my struggle having five practitioners help me to increase my business. With each practitioner, my business got worse until I didn't have any. Now that surely looked like a lack of demonstration. However, you see, it was my *perfect* demonstration, because only when I had no money left did I go into this work. I suppose if my business had prospered, this work would have been delayed, or even prevented, in this lifetime.

So it is that many people come to us for help, but they have a definite idea of what it is that they want. They have a definite idea of how harmony should appear in their experience, and sometimes even *when*. However, you see that really is not a part of our ministry. We do not aim at having instantaneous healings. They're wonderful when

they take place, if they fulfil their spiritual mission; but
that is not our object.

Our object is the changing of consciousness—the
changing of an individual's consciousness from a material
sense of life to the spiritual awareness of life; from a
material sense of religion to a spiritual sense of religion;
from a material sense of supply to a spiritual sense of supply. You see, we are the ones, when the right help is given,
who should be responding in accordance with God's will.
However, we fight this by having in our mind how the
demonstration should come out, and when, and to what
extent, and so on.

It is like parents who sometimes write to me for help.
Their son is responding to the military draft. Will I help
him pass and get into the draft? Another parent is desirous
of having their son flunk the draft. Now you see, you
can't pray to God both ways. A parent would soon be
writing you a letter, if their son got accepted and then got
himself injured or killed, asking, "What did you do? I
thought you were going to God for my son, and now look
what's happened to him!" No, even if they wanted it, we
couldn't do that. Our realization would not be of a man
in or out of the military; our realization would be of
Christ Identity, of God fulfilling Itself as the Life of this
individual. Then we would have to be satisfied with whatever direction that young man's path took.

Now this can never be repeated to you too often, because over and over that temptation can be there: "I must
save this person's life . . . I must restore their sanity . . .
I must bring about peace in their household." Actually,
peace may be the worst thing to have in the household for
their spiritual progress! So it is that we do not outline, we
do not desire; neither do we judge, criticize, nor condemn.

We turn completely from the human scene with its good side and its bad side and we pray for the revelation of Christ in our consciousness.

When I use the word *Christ*, understand that I mean your spiritual Identity or God's spiritual Plan for you, or spiritual Illumination. In our Christian mysticism, we use the word *Christ* to mean that which you in your true Identity are: the Son of God, the Child of God, the Offspring of God. Actually, it would make no difference if we were to say, "Reveal Buddha," because it means exactly the same thing—Enlightened One or Christ Self.

So it makes no difference what our terminology may be. When we turn within, let us realize that we are turning within to behold the spiritual Reality when humanhood is confronting us. When we have that second of spiritual realization, which in us is interpreted to mean we have beheld the very Christ of God, the very spiritual Reality of Being, this, then, touches the consciousness of the patient or student and begins to transform it.

You see, all experience is being transformed by the renewal of the mind—being renewed by the transforming of the mind. We are, in other words, changing our nature from the man of earth to the man who has his being in Christ. Now there are two of us: there is the man of earth that we are as human beings, and there is the man who has his being in Christ, which is our true Identity.

Now, I'm going to explain to you how this all happened, how humanhood is perpetuated in us and how it is overcome where spiritual identity is realized and demonstrated. This is not something you will give to your patients or your students. This something you will live with until you have actually demonstrated it in great measure. Otherwise, giving out what you haven't got will not benefit the other fellow and may deprive you. Do not give out spiritual Truth that you yourself have not attained in some measure of realization.

You have heard of subliminal perception. This was used in a form of advertising in which a message was flashed on a movie or television screen so quickly that the viewer never saw it. You never became conscious that it was taking place, either by sight or hearing, and yet all of a sudden you felt the urge to do what they told you to do. In one experiment, the audience was told, in the midst of a movie picture, to get up, go downstairs, and buy soda and popcorn. In those few minutes, sales increased 57 percent over the normal sale of popcorn and soda.

In another experiment, on television, a message was flashed: "Go to the telephone." You got up right in the middle of this interesting picture and you went to the telephone. When you got there, you wondered what you were doing and remembered that you didn't want to telephone anybody, and so you went back to your seat, not knowing that you had been acted upon. Your mind had been played upon. You had been used by the mentality of other people, and you had been made to obey their instructions.

England was offered the first opportunity to buy this idea and passed it up, deciding that it wasn't interested. It was bought in New York and experimented with and has since been dropped. So for all intents and purposes, it may amount to nothing further in the world's history. However, it's going to serve an important point, since with that I'm going to illustrate why we are human beings, why we are *kept* human beings, why we sin, why we have false appetites, why we are poor, why we are ever sick, and why we eventually die. It is all because of this very thing— *subliminal perception.*

As you go back to the early books of the Infinite Way,* you will see that it is written there that you are not responsible for any error touching your life, not even responsible for sins, for lack, for hate, for envy or jealousy. You're not responsible for a bit of that. All of that is a universal activity—the activity of that which Paul called the carnal mind. He summed it all up in that term, *the carnal mind*. Centuries later, Mrs. Eddy coined the term *mortal mind*.

If you like, you can use some of those terms, or terms that we have in the Infinite Way, like *universal belief*, or *universal hypnotism*, or *universal mesmerism*. You can use anything you like, because what is happening is that all the sins, diseases, lacks, limitations, and old age—all of this is a part of the vast universal ignorance, or call it universal mind (not the Divine Mind). The universal mind of man, the carnal mind, or the mortal mind is pumping its thoughts, its beliefs, and its theories into you and into me.

So it is, let us say, that a baby is born and before it can even think, it's placed in a draught and the next thing it has is a cold. Now it wasn't the baby's wrong thinking that gave it a cold. You can't blame it on the nurse or parents, because they weren't thinking of a cold for the baby either. However, the universal belief that getting in a draught gives a cold immediately operated in what they now call the subconscious mind, and the baby responded to it.

In the same way, every carnal thought, whether of a material, mental, moral, or financial nature—every material thought, every thought of false ambition, greed,

*See especially *The Infinite Way* and *Spiritual Interpretation of Scripture*—Ed.

lust, hate, injustice, and unkindness—not one bit of that is yours or mine. It is all part of this vast mental illusion, if you want to call it that; and yet every human being is subject to it. Each one falls for some particular phase of it at whatever happens to be their weakest point.

All of this is brought about unconsciously on our part, and probably unconsciously on anyone else's part. Now, there isn't such a person as a devil doing this to us in a personalized sense, and neither is there anybody in the world wicked enough to be capable of doing it to humanity. It is an aggregation. You might call it the sum total of everything that has happened since the days of Adam, of a selfish or personal nature, that forms everything that has come up out of the original belief in two powers—good and evil.

All of this sum total of evil is now floating around right in your room. Some of it has been brought in by nothing personal other than what we call the carnal mind. Some of it is in the room by virtue of radios or televisions that may be close by. You are not aware of it, because it's not plugged in, or audible; however, it's there and it's going through your room.

So we are responding to medical beliefs. We're responding even to theological beliefs. If you have an idea how many people are sick because of their fear of hell and damnation, or their fear of punishment, or their fear of God, all of which have been pumped into them since childhood, then you should know that all manner of theories and beliefs are just lurking in the air, and we know nothing about them. The world, knowing nothing of all this, wakes up one day and finds itself with a cold, or wakes up the next day and finds itself with indigestion, and then the next day desires a diamond that it can't afford and finally steals, and so on.

When you've worked enough with the sins of mankind, you'll find how true it is that there isn't really a sinner in all the world. I have never yet met a person who could rightly be termed a sinner from the standpoint of really and truly wanting to sin. Every single one I have ever met—every single one of any degree—has revealed, sooner or later, that whatever it is that's happening through them, they don't want any part of it—but they don't know how to be free of it.

You would say the same thing about the ills that you suffer, or the poverty that you suffer. You could say, "Certainly, I don't want any part of this. This is no part of me. This is no part of my will or my desire." Well, then, where does it come from if you aren't doing it? You have to shrug your shoulders and say, "I don't know."

Now I'm telling you: it's coming out of that same area of consciousness that may be likened to the activity of subliminal perception. It is something being whispered into your consciousness or subconscious; you know nothing about it to respond to it. That is the discovery I made that started all of this work, way far back in the early nineteen-thirties. I saw that there is no personal evil. I saw that evil is never personal and that it can be separated from any individual once they themselves have realized that the time has come.

The next step makes the healing work very easy. You see, this step makes it possible for you never to hold your patient or student in any form of condemnation, criticism, or judgment. It enables you to free everyone that comes to you, instantly, the moment you know "Why, this isn't your fault. This isn't your doing. You are not responsible for this."

Right then and there you've lifted a great load—and you don't even have to voice it; you only have to think it.

You have lifted such a load from your patient, or student, that their shoulders go back, normally, quickly. They don't know why, but they feel a sense of freedom. It is because you have lifted the burden of guilt and responsibility from their shoulders by realizing, "Why, this isn't you. This isn't a part of you. This is the carnal mind!"

Now you take the second step. Since God Is, and since God Is infinity, immortality, and eternality, and since God Is Omnipotence, the carnal mind isn't power—and it hasn't the power to express itself through us, once we have realized God as the only Power. The carnal mind can only operate in the consciousness of a person who has "two" powers, consciously or unconsciously—until they consciously renounce the power of evil and recognize it as a nonpower. Otherwise it will operate in them.

The very moment that you come along and realize that the carnal mind with its sum total of evil—sin, disease, death, lack, limitation, age—is a nonpower, is only an illusory belief in the mind, the universal mind, but not in your mind or mine, it is then not a power. It exists the way $2 \times 2 = 5$ exists. You see, $2 \times 2 = 5$ is a tremendous power in the mind of the person who believes it, because they're always going to give out five for four, and in the end they'll be broke. However, once it is recognized that $2 \times 2 = 5$ is *not* an entity or an identity or a substance or a law, it's nothingness. You're free and your patient is free.

Now, at this stage of your spiritual unfoldment, if the carnal mind, or somebody operating subliminal perception, were to tell you to do this, that, or the other thing, do you know that you wouldn't do it? You already know enough of the one Mind so that you would not respond to that suggestion.

Even at this point, there are very many things for which

this universal mind cannot find outlet through you. You are already at the point where you cannot be tempted to fall for many things that this world is falling for. You can't even be tempted to *fear*. You can't be tempted to fear a war. You can't be tempted to fear bombs. You can't be tempted to fear the next bit of infection or contagion or epidemic that you read about in the newspapers.

In other words, the carnal mind has already lost a great deal of its power over you. If you were awakened in the morning and found yourself completely without funds, I doubt that you could be frightened, because somewhere the thought would come, "It makes no difference, God's manna falls every day. God's Grace is my sufficiency," and there would be no fear. Just think what would happen to the person not knowing this, who believed that lack was an actual condition.

I am sure that most of you are already at a stage where you very seldom if ever have a cold or grippe or flu or some of these ailments that are common to people through bad weather. I've already perceived, since my trip to London, that we do not have the proportion of rheumatism that is reported in the healing circles of England.

When you speak to these healers, evangelical healers, and so forth, you find out that 80 percent of all the people that come to them are just crippled with rheumatism. Well, I haven't noticed any 80 percent in any of our metaphysical meetings or classes or lectures. It shows you are, to that degree, free of the mesmeric suggestion that weather or climate has to produce these terrible rheumatic claims.

So it lies within your power to attain 80 to 90 percent freedom—and probably, ultimately, 100 percent, and we'll watch for that; but at least 80 to 90 percent right now. Recognize this: as of this moment, the carnal mind cannot find outlet through you or inlet to you, since in your true Being, in your Christhood, you are One with God. It is the impartations from God that constitute your bread, your wine, your water, your substance, your resurrection, the harmony of your being.

In other words, I am consciously One with God and all that the Father hath is mine, and only that which Is of the Father is mine. I am an instrument through which God appears on earth. There is no "me"; that which you identify as me is God appearing *as* me. It is the Life of God, the Soul of God, the Mind of God, the Reality of God, the Allness of God, made individually manifest.

My oneness with God constitutes my oneness with the Mind that was in Christ Jesus, with the very Soul that is God. I am the inlet and the outlet for all that is heavenly and divine, and *only* that which is heavenly and divine. *"The devil cometh and findeth nothing in me,"* says the Master. Mortal mind, or carnal mind, may present itself to me, but I am not home to it. I do not receive it or respond to it. I do not hear it, taste it, touch it, or smell it, for that which constitutes the carnal or mortal mind is not entity or identity, but illusory belief, appearance.

You might call it temptation. This picture of mortality that presents itself to me is a temptation for me to believe in the entity and identity and reality of mortal creation. All this can be traced to the second chapter of Genesis. You see, in the first chapter you have God's pure creation. However, in the second chapter you have the creation of the carnal mind, including man, through whom temptation can operate. The man of the second chapter of Genesis is the human being, or what Paul called the man of earth, who must die. Now, the man made in the image and likeness of God, constituted of all God's qualities: that is the man who has his Being in Christ.

When you determine that "I shall live by the Grace of God, not by external things or persons," that "the Grace of God Is my sufficiency," and that "in the Presence of God Is my fullness of life, and I no longer am dependent on man whose breath is in his nostrils, and I am no longer dependent on thoughts or things since I am consciously One with my Creative Principle—God, Spirit," then your life is spiritually governed, spiritually guided, spiritually fed, and spiritually lived. From the moment that you recognize that all error is impersonal, never blame a person for any form of evil—yourself or anyone else.

Remember that every form of evil is as impersonal as every form of good. Never can you take credit for being good or just or benevolent or moral or honest or loyal or faithful. That's an impossibility. Whatever of such qualities we possess, they are God qualities. They represent God expressing Itself as our individual qualities, characteristics, and nature. Whatever evil may be expressing itself through you or me at any given moment is the degree in which we are accepting the carnal mind as power, and we are either ignorantly or carelessly permitting it to function in us.

That is why the Master said, *"Ye shall know the Truth and the Truth shall make you free."* You've got to know it. You have to know it consciously until the carnal mind is completely dead in you—and you have to know it constantly. This does not mean to set up two powers and start protecting yourself from one of them, or fearing one of them.

Remember, I have told you in the past that in the earliest days of Christian Science, Mrs. Eddy recognized mortal mind as a term denoting nothingness. It was only afterwards that students began to look on mortal mind as if it were a power to be afraid of. They began to say,

"Look what mortal mind is doing to me," or "Can you give me some protection from mortal mind, today?" Do you follow that? So mortal mind became the same power that, in religious circles, the devil had.

The enlightened Christian Scientist of today, the one who is still doing good healing work, is one who has never lost sight of the fact that mortal mind isn't a power but a term denoting nothingness; not something to be fought or overcome or risen above or destroyed. There aren't many such healers because that term, *mortal mind*, has fooled so many, and where that hasn't fooled them, personalizing error has. So that you find some who fear Roman Catholicism, you find some who fear Judaism, some who fear Orientalism, and some who fear Communism. By personalizing it, they have made themselves victims of it.

It is the same as if you were to go around fearing that you might steal. Just keep fearing enough and you probably would succumb sooner or later! Just drive a car fearing an accident long enough and I'm sure you can coax yourself into one. So it is, if you personalize error in any form: you are making yourself a victim of it, as well as your patients and students. That's why it is an error to say to a patient or student, "You must be more loving," or "You must be more forgiving," or "You must be more grateful." That's all nonsense, because that is personalizing the error.

If you find that your patient is not loving, is not kind, is not gentle, is not spiritual, then relieve your patient of that burden by realizing, "These negative qualities don't belong to you. They're part of the carnal mind, and the carnal mind is the arm of flesh—nothing." Free your patient; don't hold them in bondage.

How often it happens that a patient says, "My trouble

is sensuality," or the practitioner says, "I've discerned that you're too sensual." Now you see, that just pins it onto the individual and makes healing an impossibility. If you do detect those things, then it's only a sign that this individual is being handled by that subliminal perception, that universal or carnal mind, in that way. Then realize that this is an attribute of nothingness, or the carnal mind. It cannot use the Child of God as an avenue, as a channel, or as an instrument, because it's a nothingness itself—no presence, no power, no law to sustain any such thing.

Recognizing the fact that a human being is only a human being because the carnal mind is pumping itself into them and through them, and is being accepted as a power, you know how to die daily to your humanhood: that is, by being very sure in the morning, and certainly at night before sleeping, that the so-called theories, opinions, beliefs—the whole of the carnal mind—are not a power. The carnal mind has no avenue of expression, no law to sustain it or maintain it.

I am One with God. I and my Father Are One, and the qualities of God constitute my qualities. I am an instrument and an avenue through which, and as which, God appears on earth. The Intelligence of God, and the Love of God, and the Wisdom of God, and the Grace of God —all of this finds expression in me, through me, as me, to all of this world, for I and the Father are One!

CHAPTER 6

My True Identity

I AM INVISIBLE. You have never seen me. You have only seen your, or the world's, concept of my body. *Me* you haven't seen, for I am hiding behind my eyes. I have never seen you. I see out there only forms. I can't see you, because you're behind those eyes looking out at me, and I can't see behind your eyes. That's where you are—not inside your skull, but looking through those eyes.

Now if you have pondered in meditation this idea: "Who am I? What am I? I do not exist in my feet. I do not exist in my knees, in my stomach, my chest, my head," then where do *I* exist? I search myself from toe-nails to the topmost of my hair and I cannot find *me*. I ponder and ponder, "What is this mystery of my true identity? Why is it I have always thought I was either *of* this body or *in* this body? Now I perceive that I am not of this body and I never was in this body. I never *could* be encompassed in a body."

As you ponder that in meditation, sooner or later God will reveal to you the secret of that *I*—how you exist, and where, and when. Then you will know why I say, "Thou

art the Christ, the Son of the living God." It is not you
that I am looking at but Thou, the *I* that you are—that
which is looking out at me, that which is invisible. That
is why I cannot visualize it and that is why I cannot imagine what you look like. I don't know what your form is.
I do not know what your character or nature is as I look
out.

When I retire into the *I* that I really am, I can commune
with you. I cannot see you with my eyes, and that is why
I can't describe you. But I know you. I can tabernacle with
you, I can commune with you, I can even talk with you.
You may be ten thousand miles away, but I can still be
communing with you because the *I* of you and the *I* of me
Is all Omnipresence. Where *I am*, thou art. Wherever thou
art, *I am*, for I am in you and you are in me, and we are
in God, for we are One.

You see, for all those difficult passages of Scripture,
*omnipresence is the word, and omnipresence of I. I am
here and I am there. The Kingdom of God is neither lo
here nor lo there, but I am here and I am there. I am
everywhere. I am in and I am out, within and without, for
I Am Omnipresence. When I sit down, forget your humanhood; then I can tabernacle with your spiritual
Selfhood—because spiritually We Are One!*

Now if I were to try to pin the virtues of Christhood on
your humanhood, I would fail. But as long as I understand that the *I* of my true identity is invisible, incorporeal
omnipresence, then of course I know that that is true
about you, even if I cannot draw a picture of it. So, when
you are thinking of your cat, your dog, your bird, your
berry patch, your fruit trees, your patients, and your students, do not try to visualize them and do not try to pin
spirituality on them, for you can't. Spirituality is their true
identity, but do not finitize, do not try to picture it, and

do not try to pin it on a person. Do not try to send your thought to a person, for then you are indulging only in mental telepathy.

It is an important point of our teaching that in our meditations we must not enter the thought of our patients or students. That would be mental interference. We are not supposed to be functioning on the human plane of the mind. What we should be doing is tabernacling with God, within our consciousness. When we are doing that, there is then a spiritual bond between all of us, a spiritual contact; but it has in it nothing of a personal or finite nature.

That brings us to an important point. Centuries ago, there was no education for the people of the world. Education was restricted only to those of the Church. In those days, you would not have learned how to read and write unless you accepted an appointment to a monastery or convent. However, in those days men could go to a monastery and sign up for the Church. If they did that, they could receive whatever education there was to be had, whatever was available—though it was available only to those.

That is why, when people had letters or messages to send to one another, they had to go out and find somebody who knew how to write and do it for them. There probably was never more than one in any community— certainly not more than one in a small community. As the centuries rolled on, this broadened out a bit to where people of other importance—the government, commerce, the military—could receive some measure of education. It was the people of the government, of the Church, of the military, and of commerce who became the titled people of those days. They were titled for their services, either in the church, or the military, or the government, or (sometimes) in commerce. They then had that avenue of education opened to them.

As time has gone on and consciousness has developed, we find education available to anybody and to everybody. In the United States, we have education all the way up from kindergarten to the universities, without any charge or payment. We do have colleges and universities where parents pay tuition, but we also have just as many good ones where the student does not pay—where the community or the state pays.

Now in these monasteries, Truth was taught, as well as other things; but Truth was the major subject, more especially as philosophy developed. With these teachings there came into existence what was called Brotherhoods—religious Brotherhoods. You read in Scripture of Melchizedek, and today we read of the Essenes.

There were others, some of which were called White Brotherhoods. These White Brotherhoods were made up of spiritual students who had attained a certain degree of Enlightenment. They weren't open to every member of the monastery, they weren't open to every spiritual student. It required a certain degree of spiritual attainment and spiritual enlightenment.

Then very soon something else evolved that was called the Black Brotherhood. Wherever there were White Brotherhoods, Black Brotherhoods also sprang up. It seems strange, but all the Black Brotherhoods were made up from members of the White Brotherhoods who had gone wrong.

It is for this reason that you have sometimes heard that it is unwise to give Truth to everybody, because it's dangerous. In some cases, it is. The danger does not come from the impartation of Truth. The danger comes in giving Truth to those who are not sufficiently spiritually prepared, and, of course, you can't always know who they are.

In spiritual Truth and that which constitutes your membership in the White Brotherhood, your integrity is of such a nature that personal sense does not enter into your ministry. For instance, you will not use the Truth that you know for personal motives, whether of name, fame, or wealth. To those sufficiently enlightened, it is even nonsensical to mention this because they do not have the capacity to use it for a personal nature. However, as is proven by the Black Brotherhoods, there are always those who have not attained that degree, and they can and will use what they know for their personal ends.

Remember, this knowledge is available to you if you seek it. Among the aborigines of Australia, there are not only the good people of their tribes, but also the bad ones—those to whom you can go and have your enemies cursed. You can even have your enemies killed if you like, for they have a process of producing death mentally.

In Hawaii, where they have the Kahuna system, we also had good Kahunas and bad Kahunas. The good Kahunas were the spiritually enlightened who could heal, bless, and comfort. They were the ones who really were responsible for the maintenance of the moral and physical health and integrity of the Islands. However, there were the bad Kahunas, to whom you could go and have your enemies cursed—and you could have them killed.

In the United States, in Pennsylvania, we have a group of people who are called Hexas. You can go to them and get love potions, and if the lady doesn't want you, one of these love potions will change her mind quickly. If one of the ladies feels she wants some man and he says no, the love potions will change his mind. If not, you just tell your Hexa and they'll see to it that he dies quickly.

In other words, throughout this entire world, whether you are in Europe, Asia, South America, North America, Australia, or Africa, there is always that which is called witchcraft and sorcery. It always has been and it always will be. It is a misuse of mental powers.

Now those of you who are familiar with the history of Christian Science will remember that Mrs. Eddy treated with mental treatments and healed, but then discovered that some of her students were giving mental treatments to make people sick again so that they would come back and need another treatment. Other nasty things they also did through the misapplied power of the mind.

It is for that reason Mrs. Eddy has written in one of her writings that the same mind that can do good, can do evil. While you're on the human plane of using the mind, that is true. A person with good motives and good intent can sit down, and with the power of thought—with the power of their mind—they can help someone. On the other hand, there is the possibility of misuse of those powers, and that is where we get witchcraft and sorcery.

If you follow carefully the message of The Infinite Way, you will never be trapped in any of this, because we are not using the power of the mind except within ourselves to remind ourselves of the basic Truth—that is, the use of the correct letter of Truth. We do not put that into your mind, we do not project our thought to you. Over and over I warn about this. Do not project your thought to your patient. Never use the words, *you*, *he*, *she*, or *it*.

If you must know the Truth, know it within yourself and keep your mind there. Don't allow it to rove into any other person's domain. Then, if you are obedient to that and you do know these Truths—"In Thy Kingdom, Thy Presence, is the fullness of joy. Thy Grace is my sufficiency. There is but one Power, there is no law of sin, no law of disease, no law of lack"—give yourself all the treatments you want to mentally. But give them to yourself. Keep your thought within yourself.

Realize and remember all the Truth you can until you arrive at that place where your thought quiets down and you need no more thought. "Speak, Lord, thy servant heareth." Let the Spirit of God talk to you. You will then find yourself doing healing work and you will be realizing the Christ, but you will not be reaching "out there" to a person. The Christ Itself will encompass everything necessary.

As long as you are not using Truth for any gain, for any powers, for any dominion over anyone—as long as you are not permitting your thought to go "out there" to your patient—you are abiding in the principle of The Infinite Way. We are not a mental science. The only use we make of the mind, or of the letter of Truth, is for self-treatment. And it is self-treatment only for the purpose of lifting ourselves up, of pulling ourselves up by our own bootstraps, until we reach a point in consciousness where we can release the letter of Truth and wait for the Spirit of God to do the work.

Then we shall be a blessing to everyone. Then we are neither holding them in condemnation nor are we trying to benefit by them, or from them, or use them—all of which is the Black Brotherhood and leads ultimately to one's own destruction. For a while, individuals do get away with these things and they do benefit at others' expense; but in the end, they pay dearly for it. They pay sometimes in the loss of their lives and sometimes in the loss of their sanity. Ultimately, they always pay in the loss of their activity, whether it's a practice or a student body.

Here is the principle to illustrate that: To the pure, all things are pure. Therefore anyone who tries to impose upon the consciousness of one who is spiritually pure gets a rebound from it that knocks them off their feet. Your protection is your spiritual purity.

You will recall the illustration I gave earlier of Sapphira and Ananias.* The very moment that Peter impersonalized their error and said, "You didn't rob me; no, yours is an offense against God," the principle smacked back at them.

In the same way, heaven help any person who tries to enter your consciousness for gain or profit or wrong. The realization of the impersonalization of both good and evil will make it impossible for anybody to reach you. They will reach God—and God, being a principle, will return it right back at them. Be careful that you do not personalize good or evil, even when someone tries to wrong you. Hold fast to what you know: "You have not done this to me. You have done it unto God." Then let God handle it.

"Vengeance is Mine," saith the Lord. That doesn't mean that there's a God who punishes. It really means that when you violate the Divine principles, the violation destroys you, not God. When you put down $2+2=5$, mathematics does not harm you. The violation of the principle of mathematics, however, can be harmful.

In the same way, should you ever be tempted to let your thoughts stray from yourself to influence another, always remember this: you're not doing it unto them; you are doing it unto God. If they don't know this, you may get away with it; but if you ever strike one who does know it, you're finished. Don't be good for fear of punishment; but remember, we cannot violate spiritual principle when we're on the spiritual path and get away with it, more especially if we are mingling with those who understand the principles.

The Black Brotherhood can get away with what they're doing as long as they don't do it to a member of the White

*p. 47.

Brotherhood. If they do, their doom is in sight. This is not because the White Brotherhood or God will do anything to them, but because their violation of the principles, when it is done to an individual who knows the principles, will not work.

To the pure, all things are pure. As long as you remain pure in your spiritual integrity, the evils of this world will not come nigh thy dwelling place. A thousand may fall at your left and ten thousand at your right, but it will not come nigh you.

Our function is neither to bless man mentally nor to curse man mentally, but to leave man strictly alone. It is also to realize within yourself God's Grace, God's Presence, and to let those who have come to us and made themselves One with us be blessed by the Presence of God. However, this is not done by your mental jugglery but by your concrete realization of the Presence of God.

Always remember that the reason you have to go to a spiritually enlightened person for help is because no matter how much of the Bible or religion anyone may know, if they are not capable of bringing conscious realization of God, they cannot benefit you. It is the conscious realization of God's Presence that does the work. It is not what they know in their mind nor what they have read in books.

There are hundreds of thousands of people who have read all the Truth books in the world and they're not worth much as healers. Only a few are. The reason is this: healing depends not on what you know but on your conscious union with God and your ability to bring the Presence of God to light. That is the healing principle.

Anyone who enters your consciousness benefits by your living in that consciousness. That is why, when you go near the consciousness of an enlightened person, you feel it. Do you know what you are feeling? Well, it is not *them*;

what you're feeling is the actual Presence of God, which Is there. Let no one believe that any injury can come to anyone living in the consciousness of God's Presence. Let us never believe that it is our function to stray into the personal lives, and certainly not into the personal mentalities, of our patients or students.

When you have reached out to me for help, you are not a part of my human thought. My human thought never becomes a part of you, because I abide in Here, Within myself, awaiting the realization of God's Presence. Instead, I let the fact that you have reached out to me for help be the connecting link. No human thought of mine does it, none. Never do I indulge human thought in my inner work. Never have I in my life, and this you will find in the writings.

Not from the first day that I entered this work, have I ever given a treatment to anybody. Never have I used the words *you*, *he*, *she*, or *it*. My work is directed to Me, Within myself, so that I may know the Truth of Being, so that I may remind myself of Omnipresence, of Oneness, of one Power, the one Presence, the one Law, the one Life. Then I wait, and when the Presence of God is upon me, those of you who have reached out feel it.

Never do I reach out to others' thought individually or collectively. Not once. I remain Within myself. I realize that the Kingdom of God Is within me, that where I am, God is—that in His Presence Is the fullness of life. All that God Is, I am. Where God Is, I am. Where I am, God Is— and the fullness of the Godhead body, His Omnipresence, here and now, all-inclusive! Then I wait. Sometimes in a second, sometimes in five minutes, I feel the Spirit of God upon me.

Remember, no one has entered my thought, and I have not entered anyone's. I keep myself "back," because where *I* am, God is, and I am in the conscious realization of God's Presence. Naturally, everyone who brings himself to this consciousness feels *It*—not *me*.

When you are high enough in consciousness, you may even hear God say, *"This is my beloved Son, in whom I am well pleased."* You may even see the Light which is right here where *I* am. You may even see the Presence—certainly not with your physical eyes but with your inner vision, your spiritual faculties. You may actually witness what is here, where *I* am. For it Is a Presence, it Is a Power, it Is a light, it Is a Law. Therefore you may see it or you may feel it—but if none of these, of this I am sure: you will be aware, and that will enable you to sit back in quiet peaceful meditation.

Those who have had occasion to ask me for help, personally or on the telephone, or in writing, have surely noticed that I rarely answer with any statement of Truth or with what I call metaphysical clichés, such as "Oh, it isn't true" or "Don't worry about it; God will take care of it" or "You know it isn't real."

You don't hear statements like that from me. You won't find them in your letters and the reason is this: there isn't any Truth that could be said to you that *is* Truth. Nothing that could be said to you when you ask for help, or nothing that *you* could say to another when they ask for help, could ever be the Truth. So the greatest healing influence is the ability to refrain from answering a call for help with a metaphysical Truth. I say to you, "I don't feel well, give me some help," and the moment you answer, you have set up a conflict, you have joined issue. I have said negative and you have said positive, and now the battle is on.

When we see train tracks come together in the distance, when we see the sky sitting on the mountain, we don't walk along saying it isn't true, it's an illusion. The mere fact that we know it is an illusion makes it unnecessary for us to combat it. When we drive along the road on the desert and we see water up ahead of us, as we usually do when driving on the desert, we don't sit in the car and say there is no water on the road, that it's an appearance, an illusion.

It is because we know it is an illusion that we do not combat it, we do not enter into any arguments with it; we just drive on in the knowledge, in the realization, of its illusory nature. Were we either to stop the car and consider what to do about that water on the road, or to drive along with constant affirmation that it isn't real, it would only be because we were accepting the appearance of reality and were trying to do something about it.

If you have heard the tape *Thunder of Silence*, you will remember that there is a part in it where all of a sudden I say, "What is the use?" in a very disgusted sort of way. I had spent four hours on just one subject—the illusory nature of error—and had used about every example that I know to show that what is appearing as error has no existence, no substance, no law, no cause, no reality, and can't have effect. Then someone asked, "But how do you get rid of illusion?" Well, as a matter of fact, an illusion isn't a thing; it is an appearance. Once you know that it is an appearance, you *have* gotten rid of it; it is gone. It no longer exists as wetness on the road. It exists only as an appearance without substance.

The moment you know that train tracks do not come together, you don't have to get rid of the illusion. You look at those tracks and you say, "Yes, that's optical illusion," and then you get right on the train and go ahead riding. What you *don't* say is, "But now how must I get rid of the illusion?"

CHAPTER 7

Sin: Its Illusory Nature

S IN; WHAT the world calls sin; what the metaphysician calls sin—disease, lack, limitation: these, we are given to understand, have their foundation in a sense of selfhood apart from God, and they have no existence in the Kingdom of God, which is our individual being. Once it has been revealed to us that these so-called conditions exist only as appearances, there is nothing more to be done about the matter. We have done all.

So if I say to you, "I don't feel well, give me help," and you immediately come back with all the metaphysical arguments you know, then all you are trying to do is combat, enter into conflict with, or try to overcome, what I have said. Whereas instead, you should go very quietly within your own being, and realize what can be done with an illusion. Then, once you have discovered its illusory nature, what can you do about it? Why should you fear a toy serpent after you have discovered that it's a toy?

We can understand right well that I may have a toy serpent and yet I believe that it is a serpent and say, "Give me help." However, you, from the higher standpoint of your wisdom, discern that it is a toy serpent. So what should you do about it? Do nothing. Just give me that assurance, that's all, that all is well.

Do not try to combat my statement of error. Do not try to convince me of its error. Do not try to get rid of the serpent, overcome it, or destroy it. *Ye shall know the Truth, and the Truth shall make you free.* Now the truth about a toy serpent is that it is harmless. The truth about any infection or contagion is that it is harmless. Why, then, try to overcome it? Why argue with it? *Agree with thine adversary.*

So when a call comes for help, since we do know how real a discord appears to the one asking for help, the most compassionate thing we can do, the most loving thing we can do, is to say, "I will help you immediately; I will be with you immediately." Then the patient understands, right well, that you mean you are going to be with them in the realization of the nothingness of that which is troubling them. It is not that you are going to be with them in an all-night battle. It is not that you are going to be with them in an attempt to get God to do something for them. However, at the moment, from your high spiritual standpoint, you are able to discern the dryness of what appears as wet water on the road, or the true status of the train tracks that appear to be coming together and causing fright.

You see, the whole secret of spiritual work is the fact that you are looking out upon the world from *spiritual* vision, not material. Therefore you are always beholding Him as He Is. There have been tests run in magazines based on random photographs of people, some of whom were desperate characters and prison inmates, others of whom were people of very high character and prominence in different fields. The test was to determine which was which. Except by accident, you just couldn't do it. There was no way to judge correctly by appearances. The percentage of wrong guesses was tremendous. You would never believe it was possible that so many sweet, nice, people could be taken for desperate criminals and vice versa. From appearances you cannot always judge, but from knowledge you can.

So in your spiritual wisdom—a point of consciousness that you have attained through study and practice over the years—you are now looking out at this world and beholding it spiritually, not materially. You are beholding this universe as God, appearing in infinite form and variety. It does not fool you that appearances sometimes testify to vicious forms of error. Your study, your practice, your change from material consciousness to spiritual show you the Truth of the first chapter of Genesis.

You know that God is the only creative Principle of this universe. You know that God made all that was made. You know that all that God made was good. You know the infinite nature of God's being makes it utterly impossible that there should be any other form of creation except God appearing. Only God appearing, Is. All appearances to the contrary are deceitful.

Now then, probably in the beginning of your metaphysical days you made statements of this kind as metaphysical clichés you have learned, and you had learned to declare them on almost every occasion. Witness a couple of automobiles crack up on the road and then say, "There are no accidents in Divine Mind," as if making such a statement had any power. Were there the conviction of God as the only governing influence, no such statement could have been made. You would have looked right through the appearance with a smile, knowing the illusory nature of what was appearing.

Now that we are free of the belief of mental causes for physical diseases, we don't have to concern ourselves even with suppositional error, or suppositional causes, or suppositional effects. We go right to the heart of the situation and abide in God as the law of all Being, the principle of all Being, as the creative and maintaining and sustaining Influence.

However, because we live and move and have our being in that consciousness, because we dwell in the secret Place, because we live in that atmosphere of Oneness, when we are presented with an apppearance of evil, we do not have to combat it or deny it. We can look right through it and smile at it; but we can say to the one still under the belief, "I am with you, I will help you, I will be immediately with you. I will stay right by you until you have had the realization of Freedom."

Anything of an assuring nature, showing that two or three are gathered together in this realization, showing that you are standing by in your spiritual wisdom: that is love, that is compassion, that is the function of the healer. However, never enter into an argument with the error, or with the claim of error, or with the individual momentarily under the belief of it.

There is something in law to the effect that a case doesn't get into court until the issue is joined, until there has been somebody to make a positive statement and somebody to deny it. Then you've got something to go to court with. So it happens in this work. If somebody makes a statement of error and you make a statement of Truth, you've got a good case. Now you can go to court and fight it out—but there isn't any need for that.

We don't have to go to court with this work. There's nothing to argue about and no one to argue with. It's just a question of Truth and the awareness of Truth. This work consists in gaining a consciousness of Truth. It is gaining the actual spirit of Truth so that the healing work doesn't become a lot of mental back-and-forth argument. It becomes a very calm, clear, realization of God. That comes only with this inner feeling, this inner realization, of God Being.

It is for this reason that if I say to you, "I am ill; give me help," there isn't any Truth that you can declare about it that would be Truth, because there isn't any Truth about error. There is no way to correct error, because error doesn't exist. All there is, is the realization within you—and that's the healing agency. *The healing agency is the realization within you of God.* If you haven't a realization of God, there is no spiritual healing.

You may ask about the realization of God as to *what* and *why.* No, just the realization of God is enough. There is no *what* or *why* to it. *God Is.* If you ever have the realization that God Is, you will not be too concerned with what God is or how God is. The realization of God will bring its own unfoldment.

Teaching, however, is quite a different matter. In teaching, you do need a reason for your faith. You cannot say to a person in ignorance, "God Is." No; they may believe you, but that will not develop a consciousness for them. We develop a consciousness of Truth only because we have read so many books, heard so many lectures, had so many classes and so many recordings. We have been at this for so many years that gradually we have developed a consciousness of God's Presence, God's Power. But that was developed by all the things we know.

All the way back to one's Christian Science days or Unity days or any other days, right up to our present moment: all of that constitutes our present state of consciousness. So it is with those who come to us. Just saying to them, "God Is," is much like giving a college course to a grammar-school boy. He wouldn't know what to do with it. He has no power to assimilate it.

The student who comes to us and is told, "God Is," or "God is Love," just has no power to assimilate that. He has no foundation for the acceptance of that because he is living on appearances, judging by appearances, has been taught always to fear appearances or love appearances or hate appearances, depending on whether they were good ones or bad ones. So a person in the sense of living in appearances could hardly understand what we have to say about "God Is."

In the same way, very often we come in contact with medical thought, or with theological thought, and sometimes people have a very healthy interest in the subject, in what they have witnessed in their own experience. They want to know more. You'd be surprised how many times we've blocked their interest by throwing metaphysical statements at them that to us seem very clear. However, they, with their background, have no possible way of assimilating, understanding, and digesting. So it becomes necessary to use wisdom and discretion in throwing advanced metaphysical or spiritual Truth at those who have no foundation for it.

The simplest language that we can use and the simplest parables or examples that we can give as a foundation for the beginner will help build their consciousness. It would be a terrible thing to say to an ordinary religionist, coming to us for the first time, that God is not power. You'd be taking their whole foundation away. The first thing you know, you'd hear that "You have taken my Lord away!"

Of course, you'd have taken away their reliance. They are relying on something they call a power, and you say to them God is not power. In the sense that they would understand that, you wouldn't even be telling them the truth, because, in the sense that we understand it, God is not a power to be wielded, God is not a power to be used over something. In that sense, it is true that God is not a power. But then, we understand that because of the many years in which we have been reading and thinking in such terms as the nonpower or nonexistence of evil in any form.

So we have no need of a God to overcome that which has no reality. By now, we are prepared for that statement. In the same way, I still wonder how it was that I made that statement to the doctor that disease has no law, when, if there is anyone sure of the law of diseases, it must be doctors. They are dealing with the law of disease all the time. This one, evidently, had been prepared and was able to accept it; but others would surely be puzzled.

Yes, I have known one doctor who, right after that experience, came over from the mainland to Hawaii. He was a doctor who had quite a large hospital, and he studied with me. His reception of the statement that disease has no law shocked him. He specialized in tuberculosis, and he knew all the laws of tuberculosis—and they are pretty rigid ones, too, to the medical mind.

So we would be much better off using fewer words to those who come to us for help, making fewer statements —certainly less absolute ones—and rather give them the assurance of our cooperation in the realization of freedom and of harmony. Put their mind at rest and then let the Spirit take over rather than occupy them with a lot of mental statements which they might believe were going to heal them, and which we know right to begin with *don't*.

So if you say, "I have a cold," and I say, "Oh no, it isn't real," we've got a battle. If you say, "I have a cold," and I say, "All right, drop it; let me be with you," then there's a relaxation, and you feel that. "Oh, isn't that fine;

someone's going to be with me. Now in what way are they going to be with me?"

Well, if they know at least this about spiritual Truth, they know that it means that you are going to be with them in the realization of the true nature of being, the true nature of God—that you are standing by with that, and that you have no fear of the outcome. How can you fear the outcome of having the realization of God?

I suppose Jesus saw that when His comment was, "Do you believe that I can do this?" The moment when you can say, "Yes, I believe," there is a relaxation of fear. There is a feeling of confidence in someone, in someone's understanding. So too, it is a good thing to give the assurance of your help, the continuity of your help, your willingness to help, and your confidence in what you know. Impart that confidence, impart that assurance that you do know, and your confidence in *what* you know: then you have done all that is necessary.

You will find that it works even with students well along the Way. I get to a place, once in a while, where I reach out and ask for help. But heavens! I don't want anyone that I ask for help to come back at me with any metaphysical statements. I probably know them too; but they aren't doing me any good. I am sure that if you were to ask for help, no one would make a metaphysical statement that you don't know.

Now there is an exception to that. Sometimes a Truth reveals itself instantly when you are asked for help; and if your patient or student happens to have some understanding, you might pass that on to them as an unfoldment that has come to you. That is quite a different thing than just making up a statement in your head, or picking one out that you can remember, and throwing it at them. There isn't anything in your mind that is going to help anyone. However, if some impartation comes to you from the Spirit, then you can give it.

When I was practicing in Boston but coming down to New York weekends to take care of the work there, on one particular day in New York I had an appointment every twenty minutes. At four o'clock in the afternoon, I had a headache that made me think that I was in a boiler factory or had a boiler factory in me. I had an appointment with this practitioner for dinner, and I called him at his office and said, "I will never make that appointment unless you can give me some help. My head is pounding at me and I have a lot more appointments ahead." He said, "All right." I hung up the receiver, and *that fast* there wasn't a sign or trace of the headache.

It was the lifting of a shade. It was a beautiful experience. So I met him for dinner and I said, "That was so wonderful and so sudden; I am sure something must have revealed itself to you. What was it? What was behind that headache?"

"Well," he said, "you know, I really can't tell you."

I said, "What do you mean you can't tell me?"

He said, "Well, it's really deep, and I don't think you'd be ready for it."

I said, "That's good comedy," I said, "but now what is it—what are you afraid of?"

He said again, "I just don't think I ought to tell you."

I then told him, "All right, let's call off the dinner." He finally said, "No. If you feel that way about it, I'll tell you. I'll tell you exactly what came to me when you asked for help. I said to myself, 'What does he think I can do about a headache?'"

You see, there was about as complete a nonresistance, or complete a statement of "I can of my own self do nothing" as possible. There was as complete an absence of *I* as you can possibly get, because it wasn't thought up; it was spontaneous. Do you see? Now, you may not believe it, but very serious diseases can be healed in the self-same way if we can attain that same state of consciousness, or if we are living in that same state of consciousness.

This man I am talking about well knew that there wasn't anything that he could do or anything anyone needed protection from. Incidentally, his favorite way of healing was in his office when he had patients. He had a bronze elephant on his desk and he would listen to people tell their troubles, then say, "Is it true of that bronze elephant? I can't see how it could be true of your body. Your body has no more intelligence than this."

Of course, that statement won't help anybody, but that state of consciousness—that the body isn't self-acting, that the body cannot contract diseases, that the body in and of itself is dead, that the body responds to our state of consciousness—is all there is to it. You can trace that anywhere you want, from the toes to the top of your head. You'll find you have no sensation in the body unless you yourself are responsible. You yourself must be feeling; your body can't feel. *You* feel, and that interprets itself, represents itself, in the body. We've illustrated that over and over again.

Touch a person's hand and it's meaningless. Touch the *right* person's hand and it's dynamite. That is all there is to it. It isn't the hands touching that has anything to do with it. One kiss is just a kiss, and another one is more dynamite. The body has nothing to do with that whatsoever. That is our state of consciousness which is reflected in bodily reactions. Sooner or later, you will realize that it's also true about health.

Our conditions of health or ill health, on this human plane, are only reactions to the state of thought. That does not take us back to the mental science of mental cause for physical disease. It takes us back to whether or not we are in a material state of consciousness or a spiritual state of consciousness. As long as we are in the material state of consciousness, which is a belief in the power of effects, the body is subject to any form of discord. The moment we make the transition into the spiritual consciousness, in which we realize that all cause is an activity of consciousness, the body becomes free of most of its sensations.

Paul had that idea in his "He that soweth to his flesh shall of the flesh reap corruption; but he that soweth to the Spirit shall of the Spirit reap life everlasting." That's exactly the difference between material consciousness and spiritual consciousness. To reap to the flesh means to believe in substance, law, power, and reality in effects. However, to sow to the Spirit means to place all life, all substance, all cause, all continuity, all law and being, in the Spirit. Then that which appears as effect is but the effect of the Spirit.

Now to say that sensation is an activity of consciousness would be to withdraw every erroneous sensation from the body. To say that activity, movement, action, is an activity of consciousness would be to prevent the muscles from becoming paralyzed. Why? Because the activity of muscles is in consciousness. So it would be with all the organs and functions of the body.

If you sow to the flesh, you believe that heart, liver, and lungs can move in and of themselves and that they are an issue of life. Then, of course, you are in the material sense of existence and can only reap corruption: sin, disease, death. If, however, you have made the transition to the realization that consciousness is the law of being and the law of body, then you are sowing to the Spirit, and you will reap spiritual harmony.

Then, when the call comes for help, there is no use in answering with a lot of arguments and metaphysical statements, because right up here is the realization of all time: *Who convinceth me of sin?* All perfection is in consciousness, not in effects. All supply is in consciousness, not in dollar bills, or oranges, or crops. You live and move and have your being in that consciousness, and then when you are called upon for help, you don't have to go through a teaching process. The teaching process is different.

In teaching, you have to use every single word of Truth, statement of Truth, and thought of Truth you know in order to offset the material sense of existence. You have to gradually wear down and break down that material sense until it has disappeared and the spiritual transition has been made. At some point of our existence, reading or teaching moves us from sowing to the flesh to sowing to the Spirit. There comes an actual minute of transition which you would call realization. You will say, "I 'knew' that; but now I *know* it! Now I have the awareness, that inner conviction. It's different now. I know it's so."

When that takes place in the treatment, that's the moment of healing. Anytime a practitioner, regardless how little their understanding might be, came to a moment of realization on any point, a healing would take place. Any time a metaphysician sat down and thought through, read through, and pondered thoroughly any problem until a moment of realization came, that particular problem would be met. Now, if that happened often enough in their experience, they would have a moment of transition when the whole of the material scene would be wiped out and they would have the realization of God.

The moment they had the realization of God, then there would be no more need for these realizations with every call for help, just as my friend was able to say, "What does he think I can do about that?'' He was living up there in that state of consciousness where he knew that nothing could be done about nothing.

Had he not been in that state of consciousness, he would have closed his eyes and given a treatment. It might have lasted one minute or it might have lasted twenty minutes, but he would ultimately have come to a point of realization and the healing would have taken place. Since he was in that state of consciousness, the healing took place instantly.

The more you study, the more you ponder, the more you read, the more you practice, the more you meditate: the closer you come to that point of transition where you live in that consciousness. I have told this before: There was a practitioner in Los Angeles who was probably, in point of business and number of patients, the busiest practitioner in that city. A practitioner from Boston was visiting Los Angeles, heard about this man, and made an appointment to have lunch with him.

He went up to the practitioner's office at twelve o'clock noon and found the office filled. By one o'clock, people had been going and coming and the office was still filled. Inside you could hear the practitioner on the phone; there were two phones going constantly, and he was going constantly from one to the other: "I'll be with you; I'll help you. It's all right, I'll take care of it."

Finally, this practitioner came out of his office and said, "I'm sorry, I won't be able to have lunch with you today. You see, these people are waiting and the calls keep coming." The visiting practitioner saw that and left; but he called me on the phone. He said, "Joel, something is very wrong here. Can you have lunch with me?" So we went to lunch and he told me this story. Now the practitioner in question was a man with whom I shared an office, so I knew the whole story.

The visitor said, "You know, there must be something wrong with that practice, because he didn't give one of those people a treatment. Even the people who came in and had appointments he didn't give a treatment. They just came in; they didn't get a chance to talk. They just sat while he was on the phone, and when they got tired, they went out. Something is very wrong."

I said, "Oh no; nothing's wrong; you just don't understand. This man has a different kind of practice. He doesn't have any sick people in this practice." You see, he had attained that. He had an instantaneous healing of tuberculosis, and in the very last stages of tuberculosis too.

He had been very antagonistic to both God and Christian Science, but the thing that brought the healing was his reading the first chapter of *Science and Health*, the chapter on Prayer; and while he couldn't make heads or tails of it, something intrigued him. It intrigued him to such an extent he read the chapter five times in one night; and out of it he caught two things: God Is, and error isn't.

So he based his whole practice on that, and when patients came to him he would say, "Now, I'll tell you what to do. You take your Bible and rub every bit of print off of it mentally. Wipe it all off so you'll have nothing but blank pages. Then on every page you mentally print, 'God Is.' That's all the Bible is trying to tell you: that God Is. There *is* a God. Now you take *Science and Health* and wipe off every bit of print. You don't need any. Just print on each page, 'There is no error,' because that's all Mrs. Eddy was trying to say to you."

That was his secret, that was his conviction, that was his sowing to the Spirit.

CHAPTER 8

Not Good or Evil

I SUPPOSE THAT if we have a hard job to do, we might as well do it first. Let's get to the most difficult part of our work at once. Those of you who are familiar with religious literature or metaphysical literature know that all spiritual living is based on the overcoming of self; what Paul calls dying daily, being reborn of the Spirit.

The religious literature of the world is in agreement that the only devil there is, is ourselves. By "ourselves" I mean my Joel self, your Bill self, your Mary self. It is that part of you or me which insists on being catered to, that part of us which can have hurt feelings or hurt bodies, that part of us which can have fears one day and joys another day.

Now ordinarily in our physical world, you think it is quite enough if you can get rid of negative aspects of yourself. That is, you want to overcome your bad traits, sins, diseases, and the like, and hold on to all the good ones. That, in ordinary religion, is the hope. You stop being a bad human and begin becoming a good one. You stop being sick and become well. You stop your bad temper and have a good temper. However, that has no relationship to true religion or a spiritual way of life.

In the spiritual way of life, you don't have any good world any more than you have a bad world. If anyone accuses you of having a good world, you say with the Master, *Why callest thou me good? There is only One good.''* If they complain about the bad one, You can say with Paul, "The good I would, I do not, not because I am bad, but because I find a bad power in me." So we unload our bad only on the condition that we don't try to retain good, since that would only make us little better than good church-members.

Of course, in our lifetime, church—and especially the right sense of church—can be a great blessing to us. For instance, we are in church whenever we are assembled in a place for the purpose of communion with God, where two or more can be together as spiritual unfoldment takes place. You are in church when you are at a center, as long as you are there not just to be "seen of men," not to do some praying, but if you are there to be assembled in one place in order that the Spirit of God may permeate you and the Truth of God may reveal itself to you. If you are assembled there to hear the Word of God, then you are in church.

When we come together in The Infinite Way, having as our purpose this uniting in the Spirit, we do not come to worship a far-off God nor do we meet to influence God on our behalf. We come to bring ourselves into alignment with the God or spiritual laws that have always existed, exist now, and forever will exist.

So you must accept the responsibility that is yours as an Infinite Way student and realize that it is up to you, as an individual, what degree of progress you make. The degree of unfoldment that takes place *at any given time* is not up to you: some by their very natures achieve more quickly than others. But aside from that, the *acceptance* is the difficult part, because one is getting back to the overcoming of self. No one can do that for you but you.

Now suppose I were to tell you that before we came into a given room, it was blank. There was no good in that room and there was no evil in that room. The room was in a state of blankness—just nothingness. It couldn't benefit anybody or harm anybody. Now we come into the room and what do we find here? Love, cooperation, mutualness, some measure of joy—and above all things, integrity is here. How did it get here? It wasn't here before we came. We brought it with us. The place whereon thou standest is Holy ground. The place whereon I stand is Holy ground.

So as we come together, we find no antagonism, no cause for wars, for fights, for protective work. Yes, because each one of us has come in the Spirit of Love, Truth, Sharing, and Receiving from the Father—not from each other. No one would come to this study with the idea that they were going to benefit from someone else. Each would come knowing that whatever benefit was to be derived, it had to be derived from the Father within. It must be the recognition of the Father within you. Now, in that spirit, you see that we came together in Love, Harmony, Peace, and Joy.

On the other hand, we could have brought into the room antagonism, selfishness, self-interest, the desire to get, to benefit, to achieve. Then what would have happened in that room? So you have a classic example of the fact that you yourself are responsible for the atmosphere in that room. You can't give God the credit for it. The only thing that you can give credit to is the fact that you came into the room in a spirit of love and open-mindedness, and nothing else. So you can see that the responsibility of your life is upon you. Your harmony is upon you.

God is here and God's Law is here. The responsibility rests upon you and me to come into harmony with God's Law. God's Law Is Love. *Love is the fulfilling of the Law.* It doesn't mean emotion, a personal sense, or sensuality. It means the recognition of God as Individual Being. You are only loving your neighbor as yourself when you are agreeing that God Is the Individuality, Life, Mind, Soul, and Spirit of Individual Being.

First of all, that means *your* being. You Are Self-sufficient! When you use that term, *Self-sufficient*, give it a capital S, meaning you find your sufficiency in your Self, and Self means God. So you find your sufficiency in your Self, within your own being, within the God Being of you. You do not look outside to me, or to him, or to her, or to it. You find It within your own God Being!

Now in doing that, you set *me* free, because now you have no responsibility for my demonstration and no responsibility for your neighbor's demonstration. Nobody else concerns you. Each one will make their demonstration according to their own light, not according to yours. You are responsible only for *your* demonstration. This is the Truth about your family. Realize that they are Self-sufficient and stop trying to make their demonstrations. Cooperate, yes. Help, yes.

Each one of you is helping me. This Message couldn't come through except that you are drawing it through. With different students, it can be an entirely different type of Message. *You* are drawing this Message, that God may reveal Itself; and I am merely the instrument through which God is fulfilling Its need.

In that way, we cooperate with our family, neighbors, communities, nations—our brothers and sisters—but we do not cooperate in the sense of making their demonstration or being responsible for them. Our first way of cooperating is Self-sufficient: Self-maintained and Self-sustained by the inner Selfhood. You see how that clarifies the Master's teaching: *"I have meat the world knows not of."* I have all that within me; so have you. Now you come to realize that for yourself and you come to realize that for the world. This is a universal Truth, and one by one our friends wake up to Self-sufficiency.

Spiritual love takes two forms or aspects. The first and the more important is "Love thy neighbor as thyself." Through this realization of Self-sufficiency, through this realization that God Is individual Being, through this realization that God Is the Soul and the Mind and the Spirit, the Law unto all Being, this becomes the highest form of love. It is so, even as you go out into the street and behold mortality, from health to death, from infancy to old age, from saint to sinner.

You love your neighbor as yourself in that same way through the realization of "Thank you, Father! At least I know that God Is individual Being. God Is the Being of this individual—the Life, the Mind, the Soul." That is the highest form of love, the loving of your neighbor as yourself, and it means no mental or physical interference in another life, nor mental or physical healing in another unless it is sought.

The second form of love is found in Chapter 25 of Matthew: *"I was a-hungered, and ye gave me meat. I was thirsty, and ye gave me drink. I was a stranger, and ye took me in. Naked, and ye clothed me. I was sick, and ye visited me. I was in prison, and ye came to me."* "O Master, when did we do anything like that for you?" *"Inasmuch as ye did it unto one of the least of these my Brethren, ye have done it unto me."*

So it is in our experience: without trying to make a parasite of our neighbor, we still have opportunities to heal the sick, raise the dead, temporarily supply someone with food, clothing, or housing. We can provide forms of human good, not by undertaking to live people's lives for them, to control them, but by those spiritual Graces that inform us of some temporary need. We have the Grace to share and then go on about our business without any sense that we did it—because we didn't. It is God's Grace that meets one's sufficiency.

There is only one way to overcome the Joel self. Never accept your errors as though they were yours. Remember, they are impersonal errors, victimizing you. By recognizing that no quality of God's is yours, even if you know the Truth or bring out a healing, or even if you do meet their rent for them, you don't get any feeling that it was you. Whatever good is performed through us is an activity of God, for which we are just the instrument. Whatever evil we do is a temporary falling under the spell of world hypnotism.

Now it is at this point that we come to the most difficult part of overcoming the self. There is one thing we would all like to retain and that is our opinions. We all have the conviction that we are entitled to our opinions—and that, of course, is the last stand of the devil self; because we are *not* entitled to our opinions.

We are not permitted to judge. Now one-half of that isn't too difficult. You have probably already come to the place where it isn't too difficult to withdraw judgments of evil. Ordinary humans love to look outward. That way at least they can know the facts about the other fellow and know how evil he is.

However, the Infinite Way student has already come to the place where he can say, "No, it is not up to me to condemn or judge, so I am withholding all judgment about this.'' As for the other half—well, we can't even judge the good. We can't even look at a healthy person and say they are good and healthy. We cannot judge, we cannot have an opinion, we cannot even be satisfied with good in the human picture.

So then we come to a place that determines what degree of healing work we are ever going to be able to do. If you think for a moment that you will be happy to see a sick person get well, a bad person become good, you might as well give up your hopes right now of attaining any great degree of progress in a spiritual ministry. A spiritual ministry says, ''You are spiritual: that is the actuality of your being. It is neither good nor bad, healthy nor unhealthy. The Truth of your being Is God. God Is the reality of your being.'' You dare not have any judgment other than that.

So when the patient says, ''The fever is one hundred and fourteen,'' you cannot come to the question whether it is evil and therefore you must do something about it. Also, when it is down to one hundred and one, you can't say, ''Isn't that fine?'' Rather, it is the death of selfhood when you can have no reaction to good or bad humanhood. It is the ultimate death of personal self when you no longer react to the human good or the human evil. This is the difficult part of this work; this is the difficult part of the spiritual Path. *Judge not that ye be not judged.*

You see, a doctor may come along and examine you and tell you that you are 100 percent healthy. You must be careful of that judgment because of what might happen tomorrow. You might rest in that judgment and really believe it. Many have been insured and died before the premium was due. Or it may be that a person looks at his list of investments and leans back on that. Then the bottom drops out of the market, or something else happens in the human scene, and all of a sudden they are thrown. Yes, they were judging by appearances. Do you see that?

One day we have peace in the world, the next day war in the world. One day it was the good old days, and the next day the horrible days of old. If you take undue censure of the evil and undue pleasure of the good, in either case, sooner or later, you come to trouble. However, if you keep constantly before your vision the Infinite Invisible, then you are judging righteous judgment, because you are never certain that I am good or bad, rich or poor, sick or well. Now what about the Infinite Invisible? If your faith, reliance, and hope are in the conviction of the Infinite Invisible, you will find the Infinite Invisible visibly appearing.

When you look out at a person, place, or condition and call it good or evil, you are judging by appearances, and those appearances are subject to change. However, if you look *through* the appearance to the Infinite Invisible and say, "What is the nature of the Infinite Invisible? Oh, the Infinite Invisible Is Spirit," that ends that. You don't have to come back to the human picture. It will change.

I suppose it might be like a Buddhist who has been accustomed to think in terms of the Buddha and then he has to think about the Christ. He has to change all the facial expressions. I have on my desk a book of drawings, all Chinese. The infant Christ Child is Chinese, and in all these drawings the characters are Chinese. So, for a person thinking of the Spirit of God made flesh, it is all Chinese. Those are concepts, you see. They are concepts of the Christ made evident according to our interpretation. If you were going to judge the Christ by that book, you would always be looking for it with slant eyes.

So if you are going to look at what the human world

calls health or pretty form, you will have old age, and there won't be any health there. If you keep your vision inward and don't look at the infant and say, "Isn't it wonderful," or look at the eighty-year-old person and say, "Isn't it too bad," but look to the center of their being and realize the nature of the Infinite Invisible, you can but bring to yourself and to others the true Vision. Immortality is never achieved in the outer; it Is in you. The moment you can catch the glimpse of God as the only Being, you have attained Immortality. If you expect a person to attain it, you will only accomplish longevity.

When you have seen that God Is my Life, again you have died to the selfhood called age—the running down and failure of faculties. Never try to treat you or me for health or age or wealth. Recognize the Infinite Invisible as the only age or health or wealth of man, of the capacities of man, mental or physical. You see, the body itself has no capacity. It is an instrument; but it is an instrument for your belief or for your knowledge. You can make it an instrument of belief by asking how old, and what size, and what its degree of health is. Then the body will show forth every belief in the world.

Now on the other hand, you can make a spiritual instrument of your body by saying, "God Is its strength, its age, the measure of its capacity. I can do all things through Christ which strengthens me." There is not a word about muscles and bones. "I can do all things through Christ which Is my own strength and life. I can bring forth wisdom, art, music, and literature through Christ, which Is my Spirituality or artistic capacity."

If I think I have something of my own stored up in the brain, I limit it. If I believe that my capacity is in proportion to my education and experience, I limit it. However, when I say, "The Invisible Christ Is my eternality, the In-

visible Christ Is my strength, the Invisible Christ Is my being, the Invisible Christ Is the measure of my manhood
or womanhood'': you see I have placed the entire light of
my being in my Christhood or in my Invisible Selfhood.

When you do that for yourself, it is good; and when you
begin to understand that for your neighbor, that is loving your neighbor as yourself. You are acknowledging the
same Selfhood for your neighbor as yourself, and this
works miracles for people who are in any way backward,
for subnormal children in their family, for other family
members for whose conduct we are not responsible.

However, we are responsible for our *concept* of them,
and we should say, ''I don't care whether you are well or
sick, good or bad; I am relying on your Christhood.'' In
that moment you have killed off yourself, that which feels
a personal responsibility, a sense of joy or sorrow. You
have killed that off the moment you no longer have a personal reaction of sorrow toward the subnormal, and a
reaction of good toward the supernormal. ''I disregard
both of those in the realization of your spiritual Selfhood,
and it Is perfect, it Is intact, it Is complete!'' Abide in that,
rather than take a human being and change them.

You must find what it means to live the mystic life, the
life that is consciously One with God. I am consciously
One with God only when I realize that God Is my being
and Is individual Being. Therefore I may not look at a person, a place, a circumstance, or a condition and have
any opinion other than looking through it and beholding
Spirit. I am not knowing anything or anyone good or bad.

Now the difficulty is that when someone calls up and
asks for help, instinctively you know that the condition
is evil and you want to do something about making it
good, whether declaring or meditating or getting in touch
with the Spirit. No matter what it is, your first reaction

is "Oh! here is a condition, an evil!" That is where you have to start dying daily, because you can't react that way. You can't call it good or evil; and even when they say they feel better, you can't call it good. You are still standing on the fact of Infinite Spirit, God never changing.

Now I said to begin with that this lesson is the most difficult, because if we could learn this lesson, there wouldn't be need for any others. We will be entirely dead in our selfhood and thoroughly alive in our conscious union with God when we do not judge. You see, the very fact of human nature compels us to put labels on people, things, and conditions. That is the entire story of Adam, and the labels on everything are calling some things good and some evil, some black and some white. That is the Adamic nature of us: to put these labels on appearances. You are of that nature as long as you are putting judgment on person, place, circumstance, or condition.

In proportion as we overcome the Adamic nature of our being, we no longer sit in judgment. We look through the individual and become more and more aware of our Christhood and never have any sense of our humanhood at all. You can actually commune with animals and have no sense of their animal nature at all. You can carry it further and be completely at One with all nature.

Those of you who are familiar with Jacob Boehme, the old German cobbler and mystic, know of his spiritual experience: beholding Reality in place of the natural trees and flowers. It was all a Oneness of Life. In absolute Consciousness, there is no loss of identity. I remain myself and you remain yourself; and yes, there is no place where one begins and the other ends.

This is what happens when you are working for anyone and you come to any period of stillness and then get a quickening, a relaxing. What is actually happening is that you are becoming aware of spiritual Selfhood; you are then in communion with spiritual Selfhood. You have touched their reality and found that it is well. That grows upon you so that you not only touch the reality of your patient, but later on you begin to become aware of it through others during the day. Then life is a complete communion with God, with each other.

So you are not sitting in a room full of people, but you are feeling behind the appearance that flow of Love or Peace or Communion, that something that isn't human. That is a Something, an Invisible, Intangible Flow that is just going back and forth and has nothing to do with humanhood. This is recognition of True Identity; this is communion with True Identity. That is the Realization.

And that is the realization that should exist in marriage when a couple finds something in each other deeper than external appearances. Then the marriage can be said to have been made in Heaven, and we can say, "What God has joined together, no man can put asunder." If you ever come in contact with the individual with whom you have something beyond common interest, even something deeper than religion, that is the relationship that is understood as communion with the Christ, called the "Mystic Marriage" or "Oneness." Then the relationship has gone beyond the physical and the mental into a union with the Christ.

The only thing is, that because of the language of love, most of the writers make it seem like human love and bring it down to a comparison with illustrations of human love. That is because no other language has been found to express the union between an individual and his Individual Christhood, or two people on the spiritual Path in which there is nothing of sex, sensuality, or desire.

In healing work, you find a strong attachment between

student and teacher, or practitioner and patient, and that is a spiritual bond. Because of inability to express it spiritually, it comes down to the human expression "apples on the teacher's desk," and that is a necessary thing until the communion with the Christ rises above physical levels.

So very soon, we have a way of knowing our reactions to each other without any outward expression; but that only comes with the death of the selfhood, when there is no "I" that has to say, "I am grateful." When that "I" is gone, then the realization is so pure that everything is understood without visible expression. The importance of this is that, in facing the world, you do not judge—not good or evil. Have no opinion. Now you realize IS.

As you go to your home or your room, the most natural thing in the world is that somebody is going to come to your thought that you have been helping or want help, someone that is your particular problem, and you are going to have to wait and say, "Wait a minute!"

First, *outwardly* say, "I will give you help," because they do not understand where we are in Consciousness. But *inwardly*: "What am I to do? I cannot give you help. I cannot tell that you need help. Yet, I know I am looking right at you so that I can see the appearance. It is sin, disease, lack, limitation, or death. I can see that. What am I to do with that?"

Right here, The Infinite Way gives you the help. It says that what you are looking at is not a condition; it is an appearance or a suggestion or a claim. It is a mental image in thought but not an externalized condition. It is like the water on the road in the desert. We can't deny it because there it is. We see it, but if we stop the car for a minute, we will remember The Infinite Way and say, "It is not water on the road, I can't have any opinion, I can't judge.

All I can do is see something there; but I am not allowed to judge, right or wrong. It is an appearance but not an externalized condition. I don't have to do anything about it out there on the road. I only have to do something about it inside my own being, and that something that I have to do is to know that God made all that was made and it Is good." And that ends it.

Here we are today with an evil person, condition, or disease. The first thing we do is retire within ourselves. I can't call it good or evil. So if it is neither good nor evil, what is it? All I can know about it is that "it Is." What am I looking at? Am I seeing what Is—or what appears? The minute I can agree that I am seeing an appearance, then I can disregard it, because behind that appearance is that which Is. In withholding judgment as to whether the situation is good or evil, we create within us something like a vacuum, and into that vacuum Truth rushes with the Truth about the person, situation, or condition. Truth reveals Itself as the harmony unto the situation. We call this "Judging righteous judgment."

This is an extremely difficult lesson. It was originally intended for practitioner groups. There is only one way in which you can master it, achieve its understanding, and thereby demonstrate it: read it again and again. Sometimes all of it at one reading; sometimes just a section at a time. Continue with this lesson unless its inner meaning becomes illumined for you. Miracles will take place in your experience when this lesson becomes alive within you.

God and Error

WHEN WE undertake the study of The Infinite Way, it must seem to be a difficult subject, one not easy to encompass. The reason is, we are always hitting up against more and more principles. Every time we read a book or every time we hear a tape, there are more principles and we wonder if we are ever going to get to the end of it.

As a matter of fact, it is not quite that way. There are not many principles revealed in the message of The Infinite Way. What seems to make it so involved is that each principle requires so many different ways of hearing and reading before we actually attain the consciousness of it.

For instance, one of the major principles of The Infinite Way is the nature of God. Now God, as revealed in The Infinite Way, is not to be found in the religious literature of the world. The God of The Infinite Way is a very strange God because it is a God that we cannot pray to for anything. This is because our God is not withholding anything, and if it is not withholding anything, it cannot give anything.

So right there we find ourselves in trouble. That is all there is to that particular principle: there is no God to pray to for anything because God is not withholding anything. However, if you think that anyone can possibly understand that without a year or two or three of thinking of it in a hundred different ways, you are mistaken.

You might today begin to think of the sun up in the sky and realize that the sun does not give anything. The sun is shining and it is manifesting both warmth and light. It is not giving it because it was not withholding it. It is an eternal state of being, of Isness. So you can see that to pray to the sun for light, for warmth, is nonsense! Eventually, you get to see that this is the Truth about God. God Is a state of infinite, divine Being. God Is always Being, and therefore there is no way to influence God to be more of God. Even God cannot withhold Its Godliness.

Now another facet of God is that God is Law. Everything that functions in the Kingdom of God functions under Divine Law. Whether it is mathematics or music, whether it is art or literature, whether it is the sun, moon, and stars—everything that has emanated, everything that is an expression of the consciousness of God, is under spiritual Law. Therefore in our understanding of the Nature of God, we not only have to see the Isness of God, but now we have to see the Lawfulness of God.

We could go on for dozens of pages and point out that God Is Spirit and that therefore the only Law must be spiritual. God Is Life, therefore, there must be eternality and there is no possibility of death. You can go through the Infinite Way writings and spend months just on the Nature of God. This is not because there are a lot of principles to learn. There is only one principle—the principle of the Nature of God. However, there are hundreds of facets of that Nature, and it is the study of those facets of that Nature that eventually gives us the consciousness that we can rest back in God, instead of praying to God.

In the same way, our next principle is the nature of error. Once you have comprehended the Nature of God, you do not have any error to comprehend or to understand, because there cannot be an infinity of good *and* of evil. Therefore you come to the fact that error must be illusory in nature. As we follow the Nature of God and the nature of error, we come to the realization of the impersonal nature of good and the impersonal nature of evil. So we are still on the subject of God and error. With just those two principles, think how many different ways we are approaching the subject in order to develop an actual consciousness where we come to the point of "resist not evil."

Until we come to the consciousness of "resist not evil," we are not in the practice of The Infinite Way. As long as we are using a power of God over sin, disease, death, lack, limitation, we are not in the Infinite Way practice. We are in the Infinite Way practice only when we have arrived at the state of consciousness that does not fight error or that does not try to get God to do something to error. We still have not moved away from the Nature of God and the nature of error—but see how many ramifications, how many facets, we go through to arrive at that consciousness!

It is right to say that, for the young student, this is going to be a very difficult path, because they must overcome every bit of belief or understanding that they ever had about God. They have to lose the God of the orthodox Church. They even have to lose the God of the metaphysical world. They have to come into the awareness of the God that Is—into an awareness, an actual consciousness, of the Nature of God. Then, of course, they have to violate every teaching that has ever existed, whether orthodoxy or metaphysics, as to the nature of error until they see that error is not personal.

If you see a man stealing, you cannot call him a thief, because it is not the man; it is the carnal mind, this ignorance of the Nature of God, this ignorance of the nature of error. So whether a person is sick or in sin or in poverty, it is still the impersonal carnal mind, "the arm of flesh" that we recognize to be nothingness, because it does not have its source in God.

Evil cannot have its rise in God; God is too pure to behold iniquity. God Is Love, not hate. God Is Life, not death. God Is Wholeness, not limitation. So you see that while it may take the student two, three, four, or five years of very dedicated study before they actually come into a consciousness of the Nature of God and a consciousness of the nature of error, nevertheless when they are all done, they still will have attained only those two major points.

Along with that, they will have learned something else. Without setting out to do it, they will have learned the nature of prayer, because automatically the understanding of the Nature of God stops a person from asking or demanding something of God, or trying to influence or bribe God. This alone sets a person off on a whole new angle of prayer. The thought must eventually come, "How in heaven's name, then, do I bring myself under God's Grace?"

Well, in those two, three, five years, they will find a dozen different ways before they eventually get to the ultimate where they realize that you are never going to get under God's Grace through words or thoughts. You are going to get under God's Grace only when you have gotten past words and thoughts, to the place where you just sit, in a state of receptivity, until you feel the Presence and Power of God upon you.

Now if the beginner were to try that, they would go to sleep, or would hypnotize themselves, or would develop a false faith. In other words, a beginner cannot attempt to reach God through the Silence. That can only come after you have tried every other way and have finally realized, "None of *this* is the way; *that* is the way."

By this time, when you are silent there is no danger of your going to sleep. You are wide awake, alert! There is no danger now of any false gods or occult realms. Now you know! Be still! God is not in the whirlwind. God is not in the clamor of the human mind. God is not in the words and thoughts of man's origin. God is in the still, small Voice!

You can see that it must take all of the reading matter and all of the types, just as it takes all of the years of schooling, until we come to this consciousness when all of that drops away and all we are left with is the Nature of God and the nature of error—and an inner Stillness, an inner Peace. You can understand, at this point, why the mystics had very little to say; why, eventually, they left their students and went away. This was because it all seemed such foolishness to keep repeating and repeating these same things, even if you repeated them in a hundred different ways.

These are necessary for the beginner—there is no other way for them to attain it—but it becomes unnecessary once you have released God. Once you have released God, there is no need for all these words and thoughts. Now the need is for inner quiet contemplation. Now the need is for inner introspection—just pondering this Nature of God within, communing with this Spirit within.

Along with this, the ability, after four or five years, has come to you to look out there at "this world" and completely impersonalize it. So when you are seeing good, you are saying, "Ah, I am seeing more and more of the divine Nature coming into expression." Also, when you see evil, you are not personalizing it in the Democrats or the Republicans or the Socialists or the Catholics or the Jews or anybody else, but immediately say, "Ah, yes, it's the carnal mind, the arm of flesh, nothingness."

Now you find, at this point, that life is becoming simple. As you read in the press of this big attempt to have world government without wars, you no longer say, "Ah, the United Nations is something great!" You say to yourself, "I see more and more of the divine Consciousness coming into manifestation, a greater desire for mankind to live at peace." Then you see the United Nations as just an instrument of that higher Consciousness.

When you see some part of the world still determined to have war, or you see the determination of both sides not to settle, each one wanting to have its own way, you no longer blame them; you no longer blame the leaders. Now you say, "carnal mind" and perceive that personal sense of self that wants to benefit, profit, or glorify the carnal mind. Instantly you recognize it not as something that has to be defeated or as something that we need a God-power to destroy. The moment you have recognized it as carnal mind, you have recognized it as the arm of flesh, or nothingness, and you have met it.

So a student who has seriously studied these writings and tapes for five years should be at least at the beginning of that state of consciousness which has settled down into an inner peace. That's because they can see the Nature of God and they can instantly recognize the nature of error, wherever it appears, even if it does appear as a person or a condition or a thing. Life becomes simpler, Truth becomes simpler.

Living the Truth becomes simpler because at every sign of good in the world, you have that wonderful feeling of "Here is more of the divine Consciousness coming into manifestation." At every sign of evil popping up, you just have the feeling "Aha! Dear old pal: carnal mind, the arm of flesh, or nothingness; thank God we are not going to fight it. It is nothing!" Do you see that?

I go to this length to bring this to your attention because this is where we either are or should be in our group work. After all the tapes that have given us the specific things to handle and how to handle them—and after all that is in those tapes is ingrained in our consciousness—we should be in the position that we are in with twelve times twelve. At first we had to say, two times two and two times one, one times two and one times one, and then add them up until we got one hundred and forty-four. However, now, when someone says, twelve times twelve, we say one hundred and forty-four, and we have no processes. When we say one hundred and forty-four, it includes all the processes, does it not? You could not arrive at one hundred and forty-four if you had not gone through all the processes.

Now do you see how horrible it is for a young student to say evil is not real? They have not gone through any processes. All they are doing is mouthing vain repetitions, which they have not at all proven, have not at all learned. So it is for me a horrible thing to hear young students openly voicing the most profound statements of Truth, because I know it is exactly like a parrot. A parrot, I am sure, could "learn" the laws of relativity and recite them if he had a good teacher. However, the parrot would not know a thing about them.

We have to go through every step that is outlined in these writings, recordings, and monthly letters. We have to work with them, we have to prove them principle by principle, until we eventually arrive at the state of consciousness that sees good and says, "Ah, here is not a good man, not a good plan, not a good group, and not a good religion. Here is the divine Consciousness really being lived and manifested on earth."

This is not done by personalizing it but by seeing it as God in expression. By the same token, reading or hearing about all kinds of evil in the world, we are saying, "Yes, I know thee, who thou art; I know thee, the carnal mind, the universal belief in two powers, the arm of flesh, nothingness, no power! I do not have to fight you, and I do not have to call upon God. I only have to recognize you and it is done!"

At this stage, if we have been faithful in all of our specific work, we should be able to work like this: suppose there is a warning, in the newspaper or on the air, about storms, volcanoes, cyclones, and tidal waves. By now it should be a simple thing for us, at any moment of the day or night—regardless of what else we might be doing (and we should not have to stop what we are doing)—immediately to recognize, "Thank you; I know who thou art: nothing! Carnal mind, the belief in two powers, get thee gone!" and feel that we have given it a treatment. Your recognition of its source and of its nonpower, if you have attained that consciousness of instantaneous recognition, or even if you spend an hour at it, will not make it any more real than it was in the beginning.

Suppose it comes over the air or in the paper that this

is the flu season or the polio season. Why should that
strike terror in us? Why should we have to sit down for
an hour? Why, after these years of Infinite Way study and
practices, should we not be able to say, "Ah, yes, here
comes that belief in two powers," and dismiss it?

Suppose there are threats of war. Why should we not,
at this stage of our unfoldment, be able—even if we are
about our business or our housework or taking a bath or
involved in anything else—when we get the news, say,
"Yes, but they have only temporal power," and shrug it
off?

Now I am not saying to you that a young student should
dare this. They must go through all of the processes until they have attained the consciousness. The reason is—
and never forget this point—there is a third principle: the
natural man is not under the Law of God. So it is that the
natural man, the young student, their words and thoughts
are all powerless. They have no power to nullify the appearance. They have no power to bring the Grace of God
into expression. They are still the natural man who is not
under the Law of God, neither indeed can be.

It is only when you have developed the fourth-dimensional consciousness that error is nullified. You do not
even have to voice anything! You could look at error
rolling down and smile at it, and it would fade and fall
away, if you attained the consciousness. You would not
have to fight and bring yourself to a point of realization.
If you are in the fourth-dimensional consciousness, you
could say, "What did hinder you? Pick up your bed and
walk." You cannot say this from the third-dimensional
consciousness.

That is why all these young practitioners are not achiev-
ing the healings and are wondering why, since they know
the same Truth that everybody else does. The reason is,

it is not knowing of the Truth that does it. What does it is the attaining of the fourth-dimensional consciousness of Truth. It is only when you have arrived at the place where evil is not real in your consciousness that you can do the great healing works.

Now, most of our students are not doing good work; and I am sure they must wonder why, because they have these tapes, and they attend meetings, and they know the books. They do not realize that the reason is that they have not worked with them long enough or faithfully enough to have attained that actual consciousness where they can look out here and just smile at error, knowing that it is a universal belief in two powers, not ordained of God, and therefore nothingness.

When a person conducts an Infinite Way meeting, it makes no difference whether it is a tape meeting, a healing meeting, or a Bible meeting. It is not going to be too fruitful except in proportion to their ability to look out from "up here" and see the divine Consciousness of God as the consciousness of every individual, and at the same time see all of the evil sitting "out there"—the sin, the disease, the false appetite, the lack, the limitation—as the carnal mind. Evil is not to be treated, not to be worked against, not to be fought, not to be overcome, but to be recognized as the carnal mind, a belief in two powers, the arm of flesh, nothingness.

As you sit "up here," you are not stating it, you are not declaring it—it is back here in your mind. Each time that you are aware of something beautiful out front, love coming up, friendliness coming up, gratitude coming up, there is a smile there. You are seeing it as the divine Consciousness, not as a particular person.

In the same way, you are bound to see sickness "out there." There is a load of it in every meeting: sickness, false appetites, sin, lack, limitation, unemployment. However, in proportion as you can sit "up here" and see all that and inwardly smile, "I know thee, who thou art: that universal belief in two powers, that carnal mind, the arm of flesh, nothingness," they must go out uplifted, they must go out healed—those who are receptive. That is what gives you your power—not what you are saying. It is the consciousness you have attained "back here."

It is not so important, what you are saying! Most of it is not even heard out there, and most of it could not be repeated back to you fifteen minutes later. In fact, I have heard people come out of lectures and say, "Wasn't that beautiful? Wasn't it magnificent?" Then somebody asks, "What did you get?" "Oh, well, I cannot tell you exactly." Five minutes after they get out of their chair, they could not tell you what they heard; and I suppose the lecturer must have thought, "Oh, I gave a wonderful lecture!" There are no such things as wonderful lectures. There is only the state of consciousness of the individual. When that is there, it really makes no difference what was said.

In my first year in practice, a case came to me from a tuberculosis sanitarium in New York State. It was of a girl who was in the "death shack." That is the shack out on the grounds where they place them just before they pass on, because some of those passings are very difficult and noisy. To keep them away from the other patients, they place them out there in this shack.

I was asked to take this case knowing that it was at that stage. Of course, to me it was a welcome opportunity for practice. I took it, and for three weeks I had a very rough time, because I would get a message of improvement and then a message of slipping back. Then there would come a message of great improvement: "Oh, I am sitting up today"—and then another one of sliding all the way back again. It was nip and tuck for those three weeks.

At the end of the three weeks, there was such a marked improvement that this girl was moved back to the hospital buildings, out on the veranda, where they had beds—open-air beds. Thirteen weeks later, the doctor said that the tests were negative; no more TB germs. Of course, you can imagine the girl's body by that time. She had been there three years and had been at death's door. She had almost no body left. However, thirteen weeks later she walked out of there completely healed, walked into a job, walked into a home, walked into new clothing—and a year later walked into marriage.

That was way back in 1932, and she is still an Infinite Way student. She is still married to the same man and has not known a day's sickness from the time that she came out of the hospital. She has never had to ask for help since.

The beautiful thing is that in all the years that have gone by, I have lost only one case of tuberculosis. Every case that has ever been brought to me has been met. Many, many, have come to me. Now I am not giving you this for a testimony. I am telling you this to show you that it took sixteen weeks of my working with that case to arrive at that consciousness. I have a huge carton of letters written to that girl. Every day she got a letter, for four months, and anywhere from two to twenty pages. In other words, every letter was a treatment. As for her—she did not even understand the English language. However, for me—I was putting my treatment on those papers. I was treating myself. I was educating myself. I was training myself until I arrived at the consciousness of nothingness. Do you see that?

Had I not gone through those four months with that

case, I would not have been able to take care of the tuberculosis cases I have had since, because every time one
comes now, all I can do is laugh at it. I go back to those
four months in my mind and I say, "No, it cannot happen again. It was nothing then, and it is nothing now."
However, those are not *words*; that is *consciousness*—
from actually having worked with it.

So it is that in my years of practice, I worked that way
with every claim that came to me. I just worked with it until it was met. But it could not be met until I arrived at the
state of consciousness that would meet it. It is not the
words in one of our books—everybody has the same
words in the same book. It is, however, arriving at that
state of consciousness.

You should be sure that you are handling these specific
principles. Remember, the reason you are doing it is to arrive at the state of consciousness where you look out into
this world and see only two things: divine Consciousness
being more and more manifest, and the nothingness of the
carnal mind.

CHAPTER 10

A Harmonious Universe

THERE IS an ancient Hebraic belief that when the Messiah came, He would be a great and mighty king and general, that he would free the Hebrews from the slavery of Rome, and probably even free them from the horrible influences of their own Temple, their own ecclesiastical hierarchy.

When the Messiah came—as Jesus—He said, *"I have overcome the world."*

This must have been terribly mystifying to the Hebrews, because they were still under Rome and they were still under the hierarchy of the Temple. As far as they could see, the world was just as wicked as it had been before, and certainly it was just as rough on them as it had been before. The only things that He showed forth at all in His ministry to them were some individual healings and two or three feedings, which is not really great demonstration over a three-year period, if you are judging by these outer changes.

So it is that we are very apt to think of God, or the Christ, as temporal power, and then try to send it out to

do something for us, like changing the weather or stop-
ping fires or bringing peace on earth. The longer we look
in that direction, the longer we shall fail. The function of
the activity of Christ is to transform consciousness. The
outer world is only a product, or the added things, of the
change of consciousness.

In other words, if we have come to a place of peace with
ourselves, between ourselves; if we have attained a state
of consciousness in which we manifest love to each other
—joy, gratitude, cooperation—it is only because we have
had a change of consciousness to that degree. There could
be no peace in the outer experience except in proportion
to whatever change has taken place in our own consciousness.

Instead of looking out and wondering what Truth will
do for us or what this one or that one will do for us, if we
are looking out in the sense of gratitude that we have a
contribution to make in spiritual sharing, we have had a
transformation of consciousness, and the product of that
will be peace, and love, and gratitude. However, do you
not see that this could not exist without a change of
consciousness?

That is why, very often, you have a "Peace, peace when
there is no peace." Often you may find in families or
groups where there is some temporary improvement in
that direction—less fighting, less arguing, less greed, less
lust—that the moment some strong temptation comes up,
wham! we are right back at the old state of consciousness
with the same old fights and furies; showing that we had
merely improved humanly. We had merely decided not to
fight, or we had seen that it was good to be more generous, or more sharing—but we actually had not attained
the *consciousness* of it, or there would not be a reversion.

One of the great effects of our spiritual work is to improve us humanly: we decide to be better, consciously or unconsciously, and we really try to act better; and we do. However, it is not yet our demonstration, because we have not yet attained this consciousness of love, of oneness. So it is that we accept—intellectually—that Christ the Messiah is not a temporal power; but you would be surprised how, when a great temptation comes up, we all try to grasp some God-power to do something for us and use it in the same way that we have been taught, and in which we have failed, for thousands of years.

So it is that your real work is not establishing peace on earth, not even establishing peace in your home. The work is really establishing a new state of consciousness within yourself and then watching that new state of consciousness appear as a harmonious universe.

What we have to do at this stage of our unfoldment— and really it is in two parts—is first of all never lose sight of the basic principles with which we are working. We must go back over and over again to this impersonalizing and "nothingizing." We must go back over and over again to this realization of Withinness. I will come to that again in a moment.

Now we must add to this, What is my goal? What is it I am trying to attain, or achieve? Then you come down to the actual experience of "not by might, nor by power": "I am really trying to come down to the realization of nonpower. I am really trying to achieve the realizaton that since there is no power in evil—since there is no power but the One—I am really not looking for any other power. I am not trying to attain or use another power, or bring another power to bear. I am living in the realization of One power."

Let us say, for instance, that we will visualize a flower as only a bud, then stop to think that in each minute and in each hour this bud is unfolding, eventually to disclose itself as a full-blown rose. Let us ask, Why is this happening? Invisibly, something is operating in, or through, or upon, this bud which is opening it. You may call this the power of nature, a law of nature. You can call it God, if you like. It makes no difference. Be satisfied that a law of nature is operating to open every rosebud into a full-blown rose.

Then let us ask ourselves, Is there a power that could stop a rosebud from unfolding into a rose? Has nature provided some kind of power to stop it in the middle of the process? Has anyone created a power to stop the normal force of nature from operating to bring the bud to fruition? The answer is no. There is only one power operating, one power of nature, and that is to fulfill itself.

The moment you have the rosebud in water, it will start becoming a full-blown rose. The moment you plant a rose seed in the soil in which it should be, the climate in which it should be—its natural element—a law of nature will start working in the seed and bring it finally to a bush, and then to a bud and eventually to a flower.

There is a law of nature provided for that, but there is no law of nature to stop it. You say, "Oh, but influences have prevented these things from coming to fruition." Of course they have; however, not because nature provided for that, but because human nature introduced this belief in two powers. Now we have a human experience even in our gardens—a belief of two powers operating.

If you need proof of this, all you have to do is begin to live in your garden from the consciousness of one power. With every bit of work that you do in the garden, consciously remember that regardless of the human belief in two powers, the human belief in the power of destruction (whether it is a bug destruction or any other destruction), this represents only a universal belief, but not law. Your garden is encompassed by the law of Spirit—not even the law, but the Grace. Remove your garden from under the law and bring it under Grace. However, you have to do it consciously—because everything that takes place in your experience has to be done consciously. It is your consciousness that becomes the Law or Grace.

Therefore, where is your garden? It is in consciousness. What consciousness? *My* consciousness! What is *My* consciousness? *My* consciousness Is the one spiritual Consciousness that knows but one power. Therefore my garden is embodied in *My* consciousness of one power, of one Presence, of one Substance; and now *My* consciousness is the Law or Grace unto my garden.

In your household, it is the same way. Is a household a piece of matter? Is a household made up of human beings? It is, of course—but most often in the consciousness of two powers, in the consciousness of mortality. However, since this is *My* home, it Is embodied in *My* consciousness.

Now here is the step I want to carry you to today. That word *My* has a capital M. Every time you say, *My* consciousness, please have a capital M on it. You have outgrown the metaphysical stage of two consciousnesses—a human one and a Divine one. You have made a transition in which you no longer look *up to* the I of me, but look *out from* the I of me. You no longer look up to *Jesus* saying, *"My kingdom is not of this world."* *You* are now saying, *"My* kingdom is not of this world." Your own kingdom is not of this world, because you are now capital M, and capital I.

You cannot speak to your friends and neighbors and relatives in that language. Be careful that you do not. However, you can certainly look out at your garden and say, "You are embraced in *My* consciousness, and *My* consciousness Is Christ-consciousness, because It has only one Power, one Substance, one Reality."

You can look at your home, you can look at the members of your family and you can say, "You are embraced in *My* consciousness, and *My* has a capital M, because *My* individual consciousness is not made up of two powers." I could not say, "*My* peace I give unto you," if my consciousness had two powers in it. You would not be getting anything but cold words.

If you are to be the source of peace—which means health, harmony, wholeness, completeness, supply—unto your garden and your household and your family and your patients and your students—how can you be if your consciousness is not Christ-consciousness? How could you be any better or more effective than the tradesman down the street? Why not send all your patients and students to the gas station on the corner and let the station attendant, who is very polite and kind, give the help? You don't because they are still in the belief of two powers. No matter how loving or kind or serviceable they would like to be, they cannot be, because their consciousness is made up of two powers.

Is yours?

Is your consciousness made up of two powers? To some extent, yes; but not to the degreee of your neighbor, your patient, or your student. Some measure of *My* consciousness must have become your consciousness. Some measure of Christ-consciousness must have become your consciousness in these years of your study and practice. You cannot any longer be saying to yourself, "I am human consciousness, but Jesus is Divine Consciousness." At some period the two must have united and become one, and you must now be able to say, "*My* consciousness Is Divine."

What makes it Divine? There is only one fact: that in some degree you have overcome the belief in two powers, two substances, two laws, and you have come to see that *My Grace is thy sufficiency.* Now, if you were a practitioner and a patient came to you for help, would you believe that your consciousness was their sufficiency? If you did not, you have no right to be practicing. If you think you are going to give him the name and address of a man who lived two thousand years ago, then you should not be practicing! In some measure, the realization must be brought home to you that *My* consciousness is Grace unto your experience.

My consciousness is a law of health unto your experience. *My* consciousness is a law of supply unto you, because *My* consciousness is spelled with a capital M. In other words, I have left behind me the personal life of Joel that is trying to get anything or achieve anything or accomplish anything, and there is only one Consciousness left—and that is the consciousness of The Infinite Way. There is nothing personal in it and there are no personal motives in it. There is no fame to be gotten.

I can assure you, the world is not in our lifetime going to build any monuments to any one of us. There is no fame to be gotten. There might be some censure, if the work got to be too widely known! There might be condemnation and rough times, and the falling away of a lot of students who would rather not take it. So do not look for any fame or any fortune. It will not come!

Therefore, since I have no personal ends to gain, I have a consciousness that is devoid, at least in great measure, of self or self-interest. That means it must be spiritual consciousness. Ah, but you are in the same situation! When you look into your garden, or into your home, you have nothing to gain if you have a beautiful garden or a beautiful home. Those who will witness your garden, those who will live in your household or visit it will be the ones to receive the greatest blessings. You will only be an onlooker, and strangely enough, you will derive no satisfaction from it.

That was brought home during a class when quite a few students wrote and said, "What a great satisfaction it must be to you to witness the work and the improvement in the students." I realized how nonsensical that really was. There was not a sign or trace of satisfaction in it, or pleasure, and there could not be because there would have to be a person there getting credit for something good. Now how could that be?

Once you see that all of this is the working of the Spirit, nobody can stand up there and have satisfaction in seeing what the Spirit does. You might have satisfaction in knowing that the world is benefiting by the Spirit; however, there would be no *personal* sense of satisfaction. So when you see your garden in full bloom, you will not be able to take pride in it, because by then you will have realized that the reason it is in such beautiful bloom is that there was a law of One power. It is because your consciousness was devoid of the belief in two powers—but even that you could not take credit for.

Do you see, there is a place, there is a time, there is a moment of transition like there was for Saul of Tarsus when he became Paul, or Abram when he became Abraham. You notice that in the spiritual life, the name of a person changes with their higher consciousness. It always follows that the name changes, because the name that we identify ourselves with typifies our state of consciousness.

But not the family name. Whether our name is Goldsmith or Jones or Brown or Smith, it has nothing to do with us individually. That is just a family name tacked onto us for identification. However, the name we were given—Joel, John, Mary, Susie—more or less typifies our state of consciousness, especially our state of consciousness when we were born. That is what, in many cases, indirectly led to our having that name.

Then sometimes, as we grew older and ego took over, we changed the spelling of our names to something very fancy and unusual. That typified the ego that we had developed: we were not satisfied to be Mary; it had to be Marie something-or-other, and so on. If you could see some of the funny spellings of names, you would know how twisted some personalities must have become in growing up—or their parents, if they wished those names on them.

As you come to your spiritual life, you will discover either that you were given your spiritual name at birth, or that you have no attachment to the name you were given, and you commence to identify yourself, within, by some other name. You may not outwardly adopt it: we do not want to seem odd.

Remember, even our practitioners and teachers are still wearing just everyday men's and women's clothing. We are not dolling up in robes, even though we may be robed within; however, we do not display it outwardly. We may be given a new name within, but we do not adopt it outwardly or openly. We recognize it within ourselves.

All of this means, then, that your nature has changed, your consciousness has changed. The change consists of the degree of impersonality that has entered your experience. This means the degree to which you can impersonalize evil and "nothingize" it, and the degree to which you no longer have a God of power, no longer a Messiah, that is going to go out and whip Caesar or whoever.

Now, you have a Messiah. This is important for this particular work. You have a Messiah of gentleness and peace. However, you are not trying to use It to change outer conditions. You have a communion with It, and in communion with It you are at peace within yourself. You are letting It perform Its function in life. Remember, Its function is not to destroy Caesar. Its function changes human consciousness so that no more Caesars appear on the scene, or the present Caesars decide to change their careers—not by might or power, but by *My* gentle Spirit.

You are now thinking in terms of *"My peace I give unto this world,"* but you are not sending your thought back two thousand years. You are now referring to *My* individual consciousness which is imbued with the Christ, which no longer has two powers. *My* consciousness is the law of Grace unto my garden. I can walk out in my garden, up and down among those flowers, and say, "How happy I am that you are embodied in *My* consciousness, because *My* consciousness is love, and in it there is no fear, no hate, no criticism." You take in even all the bugs that are around it and say, "I love you too. Why, I do not know; but I do, because you are part of God's Kingdom too. You are here, therefore you are here to be loved, not to be hated, not to be feared—because there are not two powers."

When you have your garden embodied in a consciousness of love, not trying to use power to destroy anything, you have a beautiful garden. When you have your household embodied in that consciousness, you have a beautiful household. When you have this globe in your consciousness, and your consciousness has in it no hate, no fear:

do you not see that you have a wonderful world? You have not done anything to Caesar. Caesar has dissolved.

You have not done anything to disease; in the presence of *My* consciousness, there is no disease. In *My* consciousness, there is no disease! Why? In *My* consciousness, there are no two powers. In *My* consciousness, there is no sin! Why? In *My* consciousness, there are no two powers. There is not a power for good and a power for evil, so we do not have a good love or an evil love in our consciousness. We only have one kind of love, and that is the love that knows no fear, no hate, no animosity—above all things, no fear! The love that has no fear! Why? Because all that exists in this world Is of God!

I know that some things and some persons appear different, but it cannot be. There can only be one God; there can only be one Creator. Therefore, in spite of appearances, I love you; and I say "love," meaning an absence of hate, of fear, of judgment, of criticism. It has nothing to do with human affection. Human affection is something different, on a different level, but love is when we are able to behold each other without judgment, without criticism, without fear. Then we love our neighbor as ourself.

It is true in our experience that when we have that kind of love, we have greater affection for each other too—on the personal level of life, a much greater affection. We cannot help it, because we cannot help loving these divine qualities that have been aroused in each other. The one thing that keeps it within due bounds is the fact that we are loving our neighbor as ourself and allowing no thought or deed of ours to bring unhappiness or distress to another. It is that which enables us to keep the affection that we hold for each other in due bounds. Without that, self would come in again, with selfishness, and self-desire. But that cannot be once we have realized the universal nature of love.

Do you see the further step that we must now take in our work, acknowledging *My* consciousness and putting capital M on *My* consciousness? Put a capital L on My *Life.* Put a capital S on My *Spirit* so that we can silently —never outwardly or openly—say, "My *Spirit* is upon you."

Put a capital M on *My* presence—"*My* presence is with you"—and be not thinking in terms of some two thousand years ago, but *My* presence: "*My* presence is with you and *My* presence is divine, because *My* presence is devoid of fear, devoid of two powers, devoid of self-interest." That is what makes it capital M—*My* spirit is upon you. Just be sure that in your Soul and in your Spirit there are not two powers, that you are not fearing any power, and that you are not holding any personal sense.

Then, silently, and sacredly, and secretly, you can say, "*My* peace I give unto you. *My* presence is with you. *My* presence goes before you to make the crooked places straight. *My* consciousness is Grace unto You." Then those who bring themselves to your consciousness find themselves blessed. Whether they bring themselves into your physical presence, whether they telephone you or write you or cable you: the very moment your name appears in their consciousness, they are in your consciousness; they have united with you the minute they have thought your name. From that moment, they are in your consciousness. But what consciousness is that? It is capital M: *My* consciousness. Do you see that? That is why, even though you may not answer the telephone and you may not receive the cable, they will still receive the fruitage

—because they did not have to enter human consciousness to get spiritual healing. They entered *My* consciousness.

In the exercise of going from head to feet, feet back to head, we find that *I* am not in my body. Now where am *I*? I can only exist as Omnipresence. There is only one *I*, and that is God, and I am *I*; therefore, I exist as Omnipresence. So every time you think the name Joel, you will have already entered my consciousness, even if you were in your home, even if you were in the mountains, the desert, or on the sea. The moment you have thought my name, you have entered my consciousness, because *I* am where You are all times.

I am closer to you than your breathing, at all times, because *I* do not live as a person seeking to make a personal life. *I* live only in the realization of one Life, one Mind, one Soul, one Consciousness. *I* am that, and I am the *I* that is closer to you than breathing, nearer than hands and feet, in proportion as I have no fear of sin, of disease, of lack. The moment fear of sin, disease, or lack enters my consciousness—and that means criticism, judgment, or condemnation of it—I am no longer capital M, *My*; and in that degree I am no longer a healer. Do you see that?

The moment that personal sense would enter my consciousness and I wanted personal benefit, I would no longer be *I*, I would no longer be capital M, *My*. No! Personal sense must be absent, and fear of sin, disease, death, lack, and limitation must be absent. In that degree, *My* consciousness Is the divine Consciousness, and so Is yours in whatever degree you attain of this impersonality and this lack of fear. You see, this work brings us into a whole new consciousness, where we do not look *up at* any *I* or God or Messiah, but look *out from* the consciousness which *I Am*! That is it!

CHAPTER II

"Joint Heir"

THERE IS nothing quite as practical as the spiritual or mystical life, although the world has not yet completely awakened to this truth. There are tens of thousands, probably hundreds of thousands, now in the world who have actually experienced that the spiritual life is the most practical way of living—from every practical standpoint.

You can imagine my joy at learning that an auto sales-managers' clinic was held at Michigan State University and that the professor conducting the clinic recommended *The Contemplative Life* as a textbook for automobile salesmen. This is really a recognition of the practicality of the spiritual life. I don't mind telling you that I live with *The Contemplative Life* morning, noon, and night; and sometimes I get up in the middle of the night to be sure that I haven't overlooked something in it. I haven't, though, discovered anything about selling automobiles—at least not directly.

So it is in our work, in the business world and the professional world, in our activities with corporations, in their labor-relations problems, in the experience of students in their own business or professional lives: we have discovered and proven that there is nothing as practical as this spiritual life. If you would prove this for yourself, then be sure that you know what the principle is that you are trying to prove. Be sure that you know what it is that makes this the most practical way of life.

Our work is based, first of all, on the unfoldment given to me that God constitutes our individual being. God is the life of us, God is the mind of us, God is the soul of us. Eventually we discover that even our body is the temple of God. In the unfolding of this there came a revelation, let's say. It was such at the time, and it has proven to be a very important one—namely, that the word *consciousness* contains the entire secret of life. Certainly, it contains the secret of life as we live it in The Infinite Way.

However, I am sure you will discover that there is not one way of life for some and another way of life for others, because life Is God, and therefore there can only be one way. *Consciousness* is that way. In order to understand life, and in order to understand the spiritual way of life, it is first necessary to understand that the very nature of God is consciousness, and therefore the very nature of man is that same consciousness; for I and the Father are one.

Let us for a moment take the word *I*. Now as I say the word *I*, I mean I, Joel. You take the *I* and *your* first name. We are dealing with identity—what we mean when we say, "I, Joel," or your name. Now, very often we look in the mirror and we say, "I don't look well today," or "I *do* look well today," and thereby we make a mistake: because we cannot see ourselves in the mirror. What we see is our body but not our self.

Our self is looking out through the eyes at the body, and we cannot see our self. We cannot see I, Joel. All that we

can see is Joel's body, your body. However, the self of
you which is looking out through the eyes is something
quite different from your body, because when you say,
"I," you are not merely referring to five-feet-something,
or six-feet-something, or so many pounds of weight. You
are speaking of something that involves integrity, loyalty,
fidelity, love, joy, life, character—and none of this is apparent in the body. All of it is embodied in that part of
you, and of me, which we call "I."

I embody certain qualities, certain quantities, certain
characteristics—and on the human level, this I that I am
is limited, finite. It is limited in education, limited in
finances, limited in scope of experience—it is probably
even limited in integrity, loyalty, fidelity—and the reason
it is limited is that this human sense of "I" is being influenced by family life, environment, education or lack
of education, religion or lack of religion. All of the handi-
caps of human experience focus themselves in that human
sense of "I" and limit us. Eventually we say, "How *could*
I make good? I was limited in environment, I was limited
in education, I was limited in finances!"

Of course, we weren't looking around at that moment
to see how many people had come out of the ghetto and
made good, and how many others with no education had
made good, and so on. As long as we think of ourselves
from that human standpoint, we are thinking of ourselves
from a standpoint of limitation, and that standpoint of
limitation governs us, controls us, and influences us. Now
let us change the picture and go back to the teaching of
the Master.

*I and My Father are one. Thou seest me, thou seest the
Father that sent me, for I and the Father are One.* At first
this is difficult to believe. It is for this reason that many
generations of people have found it easy to accept the fact,

as they were mistakenly taught, that only Jesus was one with the Father, that He was the exception to the rule. This is in spite of the fact that centuries before Jesus, Moses had also declared, "I am that *I am*." The Master Himself declared, *"Before Abraham was, I am."*

Now as you begin to identify yourself with the teaching of the Master, you will begin to see that the word *I* has a far greater meaning. Even when you say, "I, Joel," or "I, [your name]," you will see that it has a far greater significance than you had believed, because if I and the Father are one, we can begin to understand Bible passages like *"Son, thou art ever with me and all that I have Is thine,"* or *"joint heir with Christ in God."*

See how this breaks down that limitation of the personal sense of self, if you can accept the Master's term *"joint heir with Christ in God"*—because it means joint heir in the heavenly riches. What are the heavenly riches? Of what is the Kingdom of God formed? What does the Kingdom of God consist of? You will remember the Master's saying, *"Take no thought for your life, what ye shall eat, what ye shall drink, wherewithal ye shall be clothed; but seek ye the Kingdom of God."*

Here, really, is a specific teaching of the spiritual way of life. Seek ye the Kingdom of God: *why*? When you discover the nature of the Kingdom of God, you will know to what you are joint heir. You will know what the heavenly riches are that you inherit by virtue of divine sonship. Without knowing the nature of the Kingdom of God, how can you know what it is that you have inherited?

The Kingdom of God is not made up of money or food or clothing or housing. The Kingdom of God is purely spiritual. There is no way to demonstrate money or houses or automobiles through the Kingdom of God. The only thing possible to demonstrate is that of which the Kingdom of God is composed. Then, of course, it becomes necessary to learn what this Kingdom of God is to which I am joint heir.

God is spirit. No one doubts this. Even those who have tried to make physical or mental images of God agree that God is spirit, and that in making these images they are merely trying to symbolize God. The Kingdom of God is spiritual, and all that goes to make up the Kingdom of God is spiritual. Then all that we are heir to is that which is embodied in spirit and composed or formed of spirit. As you search the Scriptures, remember it takes a measure of spiritual discernment even to find in Scripture what you are looking for, because the things of God must be spiritually discerned.

Searching Scripture, you discover that God is Omniscient. This means all wisdom. It is easy, isn't it, to realize that the nature of wisdom is spirit, that wisdom is not a piece of matter? And yet the Master says that once you realize the nature of the Kingdom of God as wisdom, "these things are added unto you"—even those things that go to make up our lives: homes, food, clothing, and so on—these are added.

Now if Omniscience, all wisdom, is the nature of God, then remember this: all wisdom is the nature of man; for I and the Father are one, and all that the Father hath is mine. Therefore all of the wisdom that we understand to be the nature and character of God is also the nature of man.

How can you demonstrate or prove this? There is only one way. Within your own being is the source, the fount of all that God is and all that God has. The Kingdom of God, the allness of God, is within you. Therefore to draw forth God's wisdom, it is necessary to go within yourself —no other place. It is within yourself. Whatever else must be needed in the form of books, teachers, teaching, will be added to you; but the wisdom itself must come from within you.

This is true whether you are seeking new inventions, new discoveries, new designs, new religions, new religious teachings, new forms of beauty, grace, rhythm, harmony. Regardless of what is necessary in your experience, there is only one place to look for it, and that is within the Kingdom of God, which is within you.

Now you understand why meditation is the major function of the message of The Infinite Way. Without meditation, how can you go to this inner realm within you to bring forth that which you have inherited, that which has been given to you by the Grace of God? Where else will you find it if not within the Kingdom of God? Where else will you find it but within you, since the Kingdom of God is within you?

Of course, you may say that this is all predicated on accepting the teaching of Jesus Christ; but that is not quite so. Long before the days of Jesus Christ, the Buddha had introduced deep meditation into the Oriental world, into the world of India, and revealed that the Buddha mind, which means the enlightened mind, or Christ mind, is the source of all good. Therefore it is necessary, even in Buddhism, to go within and meditate and draw forth from within that which is embraced in the Kingdom of God.

Whether it is in the nature of wisdom, guidance, or direction that we would seek, we must seek it in the Kingdom of God within ourselves, because the Kingdom of God *is* within! What makes this so is the fact that the mind of God, or the consciousness of God, is the consciousness of man. *I and my Father are One*. God the Father and God the Son are the same.

It is in this same way that there has sprung up over the

centuries a sense of separation from God. People have gotten into the habit of lifting their eyes up to heaven as if God were up there. Others have taken to making pilgrimage to Mecca, to the temple of Jerusalem, and to other places of religious worship. They are hoping to find God in one of these religious places despite the Master's revelation that the Kingdom of God is not in a holy city or even in a holy temple, but within you.

This always reminds me of Rabba, the very wonderful mystic girl of Islam, who joined such a trek to Mecca because this was the holy city where one experienced God. She went along with a large crowd of people, across water, mountains, and valleys, to reach Mecca. However, as they reached the outskirts of the city, and the throng pushed forward to get into its center, this girl hung back, when all of a sudden a realization came to her. She cried out, "O, God, forgive me that I have made this journey to Mecca to find you, who so long ago found me!"

So down through the centuries we have brought upon ourselves a sense of separation from God because we have not accepted the revelation of the great mystics that this Kingdom of God is within us. It is not only the Buddhist mystics, not only the Christian mystics, but also the Hebrew mystics who revealed that *if I mount up to heaven, Thou art there, if I make my bed in hell, Thou art there, and if I walk through the valley of the shadow of death, Thou art there!* Why? It is because we are indivisible and inseparable—for *I and the Father are One!*

Then we come to that great revelation in the word *Omnipresence.* When you think of Omnipresence, you naturally think of God as all presence, somehow or other leaving yourself out. However, Omnipresence—because I and the Father are one—means that *I also* am Omnipresence. God is the very Omnipresence of the I that I am.

I am constituted of the Omnipresence of God because I am inseparable and indivisible from God. I and my Father are One! Therefore the place whereon thou standest Is holy ground because of Omnipresence. Always remember that the Omnipresence of God means *Omnipresence where I am*—for I and the Father are one, and this makes us inseparable, indivisible.

So we come to the third: Omnipotence, all power. Do you know that each and every one of us agrees that God is Omnipotence, all power? However, how many of us have thought that the Omnipotence of God is also here where I am and embodied in the I that I am? This I that I am declaring is partaking of Omnipotence. I do not have to go somewhere for Omnipotence nor do I have to draw Omnipotence to me. Rather, I must know the Truth that I and the Father are one and that therefore the Omnipotence of God is the Omnipotence embodied in my individual being—and yours; for God is no respecter of persons.

As a matter of fact, we must never forget that one of the most vital passages given us by the Master is the one in which He says, *"Call no man on earth your Father, for One is your Father, God."* Can you accept that literally? Can you accept that God is my Father as well as the Father of Jesus? Can you accept the fact that God is my Father as well as your Father? Can you accept the fact that God is the Father of the Hebrew, the Christian, the Buddhist, the Occidental, the Oriental, the white, the black, the brown, the yellow, the red? Can you accept this? Because until you do, you cannot make the spiritual life practical. Until you discover that we are brothers and sisters, there will always be someone outside the family of God, or the household of God.

You discover on the spiritual path that it is impossible

to be dishonest. This is not because you or I may be inherently honest, but because we have discovered that we are all of the same household, the same family, and therefore we cannot cheat each other. This is regardless of who that other may be. You will also discover that on the spiritual path you cannot take up arms against your brother, regardless of how noble the cause may claim to be, because we are of one household, one family, one Being.

We have but one Father, the Creator of us all, and eventually this resolves itself into the revelation of a mystery. We are taught in Christian mysticism that we must die daily to the personal sense of self. If we do, then when we do, or even in proportion as we do, we learn a great mystery. A great mystery has resolved itself for us, and it is no longer a mystery: the self of me is the self of you. So it was this that enabled the Master to say, *"Inasmuch as ye have done it unto the least of these my brethren, ye have done it unto me."*

Now if you study the passages that come before that statement, you will discover that He says, *"When I was in prison, ye visited me, when I was sick, ye comforted me, when I was naked, ye clothed me, when I was hungry, ye fed me."* Now of course you know that Jesus was never any one of those things, and so the disciples said to Him, "When saw we Thee in prison? When saw we Thee sick? When saw we Thee naked or hungered?" He then answered them, *"Inasmuch as ye did it unto the least of these my brethren, ye did it unto me."*

In other words, the self of the man in prison, the self of the poverty-stricken man or woman in hunger or nakedness, the identity of the sick man or woman—that was me. That was my selfhood appearing as the sick, the sinning, the dying, the poor. Reading it in Scripture may not clarify that for you unless this bit of spiritual discernment comes with it so that you really can see that there is only one *I*, one Ego, one Selfhood, and this is God. That Selfhood which is God is the Selfhood of you, the Selfhood of me, regardless of who you may be or what your status may be at any given moment.

You may be the person in sin, in poverty, in disease at this particular moment, but nevertheless the identity of you is the same Selfhood that is the identity of the Master. Therefore what we do of good to one another we are doing unto the Christ. What we do of evil to one another we are doing unto the Christ, because the Christ, or Son of God, is the Selfhood of you and of me.

We who have been engaged in spiritual healing work—who have carried on some of this work in prisons and hospitals, or have carried it on in parts of Africa and India—have witnessed that it is literally true that there is a bond between all of us, regardless of our status in society or in religion, at any given moment. There is a bond between us, and that bond reveals itself only in the recognition of our spiritual identity.

Now the practical nature of this work becomes apparent when you actually discover that you cannot give away your money. On a recent trip to London, my wife and I were watching television one night and a reporter was interviewing a Scottish Lord who had just given away his second million pounds. The reporter asked, "Sir, when you give away these million pounds, don't you feel afterwards that something is missing, that you have lost something or are without something?" This gentleman laughed, really laughed out loud, and responded, "No, there is a mystery about it. I don't know the answer; but what has happened is that, as fast as I give it away, it comes right back!"

You see, if you are a philanthropist and actually believe that what you give away is yours, that may not happen. It has happened that a lot of people, out of generosity of the heart, have given away everything they had and then found themselves impoverished. However, that was because they really believed that what they gave away was theirs, and they believed that they were giving it away. Neither one of these things was true.

First of all, "the earth is the Lord's and the fullness thereof," and the sooner each one of us learns that, the better off we will be. There is no such thing as personal possession. Of course, many have not discovered that yet, but you have it to look forward to, because the day is coming when you will check your possessions at a Probate Court and then you will learn that they really weren't yours at all. No, we really have nothing of ourselves; "the earth is the Lord's and the fullness thereof."

Secondly, there is none of us quite so good, so noble, or so generous as to give away millions of dollars. If and when we do, you can be assured of this: God is operating in our consciousness, and it is God doing it through us. We must readily realize that our benevolence, whatever its degree at the present moment, is not because you or I are so good or generous or benevolent, but that God Is good and that God is expressing that good through us.

The master recognized this in His statement *"Why callest thou Me good? There is but one good: the Father in heaven."* So it is that we must first of all recognize that the earth is the Lord's and the fullness thereof; and let's not call me good, but let us recognize that the Father is working through me. This opens you to the entire subject I have been addressing: that wisdom Is God. God Is Omniscience, but the Omniscience that is God is also my individual wisdom when I turn within and recognize God's Omniscience here where I am. It is also that God's omnipotence, God's power, is the power expressing in and through me; for there is but one power as well as Omnipresence.

So now we come to the word *love*. It is impossible, in any true sense, for us to love. All that may be called human love is some form of selfishness, some degree of selfishness. There is no human love that is divine. All human love is based on a sense of self. We say we love our children, and that is selfish because we don't love the children of our neighbors, certainly not the same as we love our own children. Yet the Love of *God* is impartial. When we stop loving and let God love through us, you will discover that we do not merely provide for our children's education, but we are helping to provide for the education of some of our neighbors' children.

We do not merely provide for our family. Automatically, when we recognize that God is love, that *I* am not loving but that the Love of God is permitted to flow through me, we will soon discover that we cannot give all our income to our own family. This recognition will not permit us to do it. It compels us to provide for some of those families who at present cannot provide for themselves.

So you discover this in the realization that I and the Father are One, that the place whereon I stand Is holy ground; for it is the Mind of God that is functioning as my mind, the Life of God that is functioning as my life, the Power of God that is functioning as my power, the Presence of God that is functioning as me, and the Love of God that is flowing through me. You will discover how practical all this is, because you will have discovered the secret of supply. Supply is not that which comes to us but that which flows out through us and from us—because the Kingdom of God Is within us!

Therefore in meditation, as you turn within to the Kingdom of God that Is within you and let It flow, you will discover that intelligence is flowing, that love is flowing, that wisdom is flowing, that beauty is flowing; harmony, rhythm, color, Grace—all of this is flowing; and as it flows out from you, so does the bread that you cast upon the water flow back to you!

CHAPTER 12

The Realm of God

Can you imagine what it means to break the limitations of personal selfhood in this realization when I say "I"? I am talking about a Kingdom of God, a Realm of God, that is within me, which is my inner spiritual selfhood, and out of this *I* flows infinite capacity, infinite substance, infinite abundance, infinite wisdom, infinite love. Now what happens in this and no other way that has ever been discovered or revealed to man, is that we break what the Orientals call karmic law, and also what in Christian teaching is called "as ye sow, so shall ye reap."

Please remember that as human beings we are born into the law of "as ye sow, so shall ye reap." If you are good, goodness comes back to you, and in the degree that you are not good, something of an ungood nature comes back to you. In the Bible, back in the days of Moses and even before, it was erroneously taught that it is God that rewards you and God that punishes you. Of course, the Hebrews accepted this for generations and generations, and then finally the Christians took over that teaching and they too have made a point of it—that God rewards you and God punishes you. But there isn't a word of Truth in the entire teaching.

All of the good that comes into your experience as a human is a direct result of your own good: "as ye sow, so shall ye reap." All of the evil that comes into your experience comes back as a direct result either of the evil you have sown or the ignorance of Truth that you have accepted. It has nothing to do with God, because "God is too pure to behold iniquity."

I can also assure you of this: in the entire Kingdom of God, there is neither reward nor punishment. In the entire Kingdom of God there is no evil. In the entire Kingdom of God, there is no giving and there is no withholding—for you must understand that if there were giving, there would first have to be withholding.

In other words, if there were any such thing as the sun giving light, it would indicate that at some time or other the sun *wasn't* giving light. Now it is giving it, but tomorrow it would not give it for some reason. However, as the sun has no capacity to withhold or to give light, its only capacity is to be light. So it is that God has no capacity to give. God has no capacity to withhold. God's only capacity is to be the Light of the world.

God's capacity is to be Love, be Omniscience, be Omnipotence, be Omnipresence—never giving, never withholding. The giving and the withholding lie entirely within the realm of human experience, under that law of "as ye sow, so shall ye reap." You have Paul repeating this: "If you sow to the flesh, you will reap corruption. If you sow to the Spirit, you will reap life everlasting."

However, there is a way in which you neither sow nor reap, a way in which you also "be"—because God Is being, and God Is being you. That is when you first realize that God Is your selfhood and that there is no capacity for evil in God. There is no capacity for sin, no capacity for disease, no capacity for death. God has no pleasure in your dying. *Turn ye and live!*

There is no death in God. There is no disease in God, there is no sickness. There is no poverty in God. God Is infinite being, infinite good, divine love, all wisdom, all presence, all power. Therefore when you first acknowledge that the selfhood of God Is infinite Divine being— pure spirit—and that the selfhood of God Is your selfhood, Is the spirit within you, Is the son of God within you: you then very quickly begin to lose the capacity to do wrong. As a matter of fact, no one ever does wrong until they first think it, and you therefore lose the capacity to think it. You lose the capacity to desire that which is not rightfully yours; you lose the capacity for sin, for evil.

However, once you discover that you no longer have tendencies toward wrongdoing, you begin to realize the great mystery: now you no longer have a capacity to be good. You now recognize that the good flowing through you has nothing to do with you and that it is actually flowing *through* you. You haven't directed it, you haven't willed it. Automatically it is taking place *through* you before you ever had a chance to think about it. Then you will discover that in your daily meditations, in which you are acknowledging the presence of God within you, it is the selfhood of God in which you are relaxing in order to let God live your life.

In the words of Paul, "I live; yet not I, but Christ liveth my life." Well, at a certain point you couldn't truthfully say that. You are living your own life, and whatever you are thinking of error, you are thinking, and whatever of good you are doing, you are doing. However, eventually through your meditations you begin in very small ways to discover that good is flowing through you for which you yourself are not responsible. All of a sudden you notice that it is there, but you didn't set it in motion.

Then you will understand Paul and you will say, "Heavens, what has happened to me? I live; yet not I, but Christ is living my life. It isn't I who thought of doing this particular beneficence. It isn't I who have always been so forgiving, so loving. And now I detect something other than this that I considered myself to be. Now I understand this *I* that is God, this selfhood that is God, or the Christ. I realize there is now, alive in me, this transcendental Presence, or Power, that is living my life. Now I am no longer sowing or reaping. I am neither sowing evil nor sowing good. I am now the instrumentality through which God is living. Therefore I can accumulate no bad karma and no good karma, for I and the Father are One, and the Father's Life is living Itself. It has no bad karma, it has no good karma. It has no short life and it has no long life."

I think you will discover, as I have discovered, that in the contemplative life your attention is consciously directed to that withinness, so that in meditation you can contemplate this Presence that is within you until the mind settles down without thinking. Then up from the depths, from within you, come the revelation and the realization that it is literally true, and now demonstrably true, that I am not living my own life; Christ liveth my life.

We read in Scripture that ten righteous men can save a city. In the past hundred years, we have been proving in Christian Science, in Unity, in New Thought, and in The Infinite Way that one individual imbued with Truth can bring healing of mind, body, finances, or human relationships to thousands of people called patients or students.

Just think of some of the practitioners whom you may

have known in any of these movements—some of the very busy ones, some of the very successful ones. Think of the hundreds of people, sometimes thousands, that even one of these practitioners may have influenced for good that brought physical healing—mental, moral, and financial.

As a matter of fact, I can remember sitting in the presence of one practitioner and within three months being healed of a disease that was supposed to have killed me within those three months. I can also remember sitting in meditation with another practitioner and being so completely lifted out of my old selfhood that I never again could smoke or drink or gamble or do any of the ordinary things that were part of a businessman's life. It was this experience that led right into this spiritual work. Think, for a moment, of the influence of those two people in my own life, and then think of all the patients or students with whom they worked over a period of years.

Now what of the practitioners you have known, or any of the teachers you have known, or any of the metaphysical or spiritual writers you have known: what set them apart from the rest of mankind? What set them apart so that they could bring about these healing works of the body, of the mind, of the character, of the morals, or of the purse? What set them apart?

The answer is this: first, they were in some way—and for some reason—drawn to the study of Truth, and they began to fill their minds with Truth through books, through lectures, through teachings, through classes. Eventually, something happened within them. They probably couldn't describe to you what it was. You probably have never stopped to ask yourself what it was. However, at some particular moment in their lives they actually made a transition from being man, whose breath is in his nostrils to being that man who has his being in Christ.

In other words, at some particular moment in their experience they attained—and remember that word *attained* —some measure of that mind that was in Christ Jesus. They attained some degree of spiritual consciousness, Christ consciousness. They attained some measure of the transcendental—that which is beyond the human—and from that moment on, error, evil, sin, disease, false appetites, and lack lost their reality to them. Then as we came to them with our physical, moral, financial, or human-relationship problems, whatever the nature of the error or evil, it disappeared just as darkness leaves a room when the light is turned on.

Of course, the darkness in the room hasn't gone anywhere, because there is no such thing, no such entity, as darkness. What we call darkness is merely an absence of light. However, in the presence of light there is no darkness, nor does darkness go anywhere.

In the three-dimensional mind—that is, the mind into which we were born—sin, disease, death, lack, limitation are the realities. In fact, they are greater realities than health or harmony. However, the moment that we bring our sins and diseases and lacks into the presence of the spiritually illumined—those who have had that moment of transition—then our disease disappears, and so does our sin, our false appetite, the claim, the belief, whatever it may have been.

Remember that as long as we are only human beings, we cannot function as practitioners or spiritual teachers, because we lack that one essential. We may have the will, we may have the desire, we may have the hope—but none of those things heal, none of those things reform, none of those things enrich. It requires the actual experience of the Christ, the actual experience of spiritual illumination, the actual experience of the transcendental Presence.

When that comes to individuals, they are set apart; and in proportion to their fidelity to It, they will be successful as practitioners, healers, teachers, and the like.

First of all, this should bring to our attention that as we become students of spiritual Truth, we must be perfectly content to remain students and not try to be practitioners and teachers until that experience actually takes place within our consciousness which results in our being set apart. Those who have been with me many years recognize that experience as the one that I had while sitting in the presence of a man who himself had received such spiritual light that he was really a very great and famous healer. He never undertook teaching, because he never seemed to understand what it was that had taken place within him. He could let it take place and produce healing work; but he couldn't understand it. So I discovered, after this particular meditation with him, that people were coming to me and asking me to pray for them, and they were getting well.

In the years that have gone by since then, I have witnessed how this happens in the lives of others. I've witnessed it in Christian Science, I've witnessed it in Unity, and certainly I have been witnessing it in The Infinite Way. For a long time, in most cases, they study Truth, many of them having the desire to heal, the desire to teach, the desire to give to others—but unable to do so. I say to these, "Please be patient. You must wait until the Spirit of the Lord God Is upon you, and you are ordained to do these things."

As the Master said to His disciples when he parted from them, *"Remain in the city until you are imbued from on High, until this Spirit of the Lord Is upon you."* There is a moment, a definite moment—and everyone knows when it occurs—when this Spirit of the Lord God Is consciously upon them and working through them. Of course, the way they know it is through the experience of others who come within range of their consciousness.

The first step leading toward this is the filling of the mind, the consciousness, with Truth. The first fruitage that you will notice will be either in your family or among your neighbors and friends, when someone begins to detect that you have something that they haven't. They begin to ask you what you have or ask you to share it with them or even ask for help.

I am bringing this to your attention for a specific purpose. In ancient days, when the Spirit of the Lord God was upon one, this was called the coming of the Christ, or the first coming of Christ to earth, the first coming of Christ to the human consciousness. As you know, it happened with Moses. He was a shepherd for many years but undoubtedly within himself contemplated God and the Things of God.

In a certain moment, he meets God, face-to-face. God is revealed within his soul. God even becomes the Voice that speaks through him. From that moment on, instead of just being a shepherd of sheep, he becomes the shepherd of a whole nation of people. Without the benefit of arms, without the benefit of an army, he rescues the entire Hebrew nation right out from under the nose of Pharaoh and delivers them to the entrance of the Promised Land.

That's all that any teacher can do for a student, or a group of students: bring them to the *entrance* of the Promised Land. No teacher can take a student *into* the Promised Land. Every student has to walk into that Kingdom through their own consciousness. The function of the teacher is merely to lead them to the entrance, and then they themselves have to take over and walk through.

In the last hundred and more years, we have witnessed

that it is not only the saints, the seers, and the mystics who have received this Spirit of God. We have learned that it is possible for almost anybody and everybody to attain some measure of that Spirit of God. I am sure that had it ever been said two thousand years ago that there would be ten, eleven, twelve, thirteen, fourteen thousand people doing spiritual healing work on earth, it would have been ridiculed. It would have been believed that only those whom God visited could do that.

Now we know that God visits anybody and everybody who can open their consciousness to that Presence which is within. It is for this reason that so many of us who are merely men and women in business and in other walks of life are actually spiritual healers and spiritual teachers— for God is no respecter of persons. God is available to you and to me in the degree that we open ourselves to that Presence.

This has a meaning now far greater than anything we have heretofore realized, because up to now, we have thought of this coming of the Christ to individual consciousness as an unusual experience. It was always within the realm of the First Coming of the Christ, meaning the coming of the Christ to your individual consciousness and mind.

However, another revelation has been given to us, and we are at the beginning of this new era which we will call the Second Coming of Christ. By this we will mean not the coming of the Christ to individual you and me, who seek it, but the coming of the Christ to earth as the consciousness of all mankind! In other words, it is the consciousness into which your childen and grandchildren will be born so that they will not have to go through our experience. They will be born into their spiritual identity and spiritual demonstration.

In the past, religion has always worked with the present

generation, and even if it succeeded in taking you and me as a child or adult and leading us up to the point of spiritual consciousness, it always had to begin all over again with our children and grandchildren. We just about started to get a bit spiritual when the call came to leave this earth. Then the Church had to begin with the next generation and lead them up to that point and again witness them go on.

This will no longer be necessary as we come into the experience of the Christ. The children and grandchildren of this generation will be born into this. We will not have to begin to educate the next generation into spirituality; they will be born into It, and that will be the promised day: when the Kingdom of God is established on earth as it is in heaven, when the Kingdom of Consciousness of God is established on earth, and children are born into It.

This day is here and now. This day the Christ is being established as the universal Consciousness, and it is for this reason that you are witnessing something on earth that never before existed. That is, it is less possible now for men to do evil than it ever was before, because as they think of doing it, the repercussion is upon them. In other words, there is already enough Christ established in human consciousness that not only the doing of evil but the mere thinking of evil is enough to bring a repercussion on the thinker and the doer.

In the third-dimensional life—that life into which we were born—man could do all kinds of evil and go through life experiencing very little punishment. That is why for so many generations we have had slavery, we have had man's inhumanity to man, we have had wars. And there never has been a righteous war. Every war ever fought has been an evil one, and those who perpetrated it got off pretty easy. The sufferers were the victims.

I am asserting that less and less of that will be possible from now on—less and less of man's inhumanity to man; less of cheating men, stealing from them, robbing them of their birthright. There will be also less of sending them into wars, because the amount of Christ that is now functioning in human consciousness is sufficient to wreak immediate vengeance upon those who perpetrate wrong —not vengeance from the standpoint of the Christ, but from that of the human bringing upon himself the penalty of his thoughts, motives, and deeds.

You will remember that Judas Iscariot committed suicide shortly after his betrayal of the Master. Perhaps you do not know why he committed suicide, or what made it inevitable. Had he betrayed Pilate, he never would have had to commit suicide, and he might even have lived to enjoy his money. However, you cannot do wrong unto the Christ without its immediately having its repercussion upon you. It is not because the Christ does anything to you, but because coming into the Presence of the Christ destroys the evil. Evil destroys those who cling to it. Those who can relinquish the evil are healed.

That is why, when you and I come in sin before those of spiritual light, we are healed rather than destroyed. The reason is that we really don't want the sin that we may be indulging. Therefore, when we bring ourselves into the Presence of the Christ, we lose the sin, we lose the false appetite, and we hear the Master say, *"Neither do I condemn thee; thy sins be forgiven thee; only, sin no more lest a worse thing come upon thee."*

Or we may be the thief on the cross, but we look to the Master and He immediately says, *"I take you with me into paradise this day."* So if there is a sin, a false appetite, any evil, any wrong within our consciousness, and we are at that point where we would really like to be free of it, we need only seek someone who has attained some measure of spiritual light and we shall be forgiven our sin, our false appetite. We shall be set free.

On the other hand, if we hold within ourselves some wrong intent, wrong desire, evil motive, and we have not come to the place of wanting to be free of it but would rather like to profit from it, heaven help us if we ever hit up against anyone of spiritual light. It will not only destroy the evil, it will destroy us, who are clinging to it. That's what is taking place in the world today—not necessarily because the evildoers are hitting up against someone of spiritual light, but because there is so much spiritual light loosed in human consciousness.

Therefore, those who have in their mind the destruction of others or the enslavement of others or the impoverishment of others or the holding of others in bondage to anything—be assured they now are hitting up against the Christ that is loosed in human consciousness. They are finding their punishment long before their plan succeeds, and this is happening throughout the world.

Bring your attention to this: every bit of spiritual light that you as an individual attain increases the amount of Christ consciousness that is loosed in the world. "I, if I be lifted up, shall draw all men unto me." Therefore, if I have attained any measure at all of Christ's consciousness, you may be assured that if you are receptive and responsive, you can come away with an uplift, a physical healing—mental, moral, financial, any nature. Or you may be lifted yourself into a higher measure of Christ consciousness just by virtue of someone else's being lifted up.

When I have a group of two, three, six, twelve, who have studied for years and who have attained some measure of spiritual light, you may be assured that this light is reaching hundreds, and hundreds are being drawn to it. When we have hundreds, then thousands are being drawn to the light. This is because any measure of light in my consciousness produces a spark of light in the consciousness of any one or more of you, who are at all spiritually inclined. Therefore any measure of spiritual light that is raised up in you immediately begins to raise up some member of your family, a neighbor, a friend, a relative, or a stranger. All of this bears witness to the fact that the measure of Christ raised up in an individual is the measure of Christ loosed in consciousness to raise up others!

CHAPTER 13

Know Thy Self

W E HAVE concluded that the measure of Christ that is raised up in an individual is the measure of Christ loosed in consciousness to raise up others. Then if you have been lifted up by so much as a particle of spiritual light, you are carrying that particle out into the world. This means that any degree of sin, disease, lack, or limitation that touches your consciousness immediately starts to be dissolved, and others get healings.

But I am afraid to tell you that it also means that anyone who comes into the orbit of your experience clinging to the desire to do evil is apt to find themselves getting ready for a funeral, because coming into contact with the Christ of your consciousness will do to them what it did unto Judas Iscariot. If Judas will not let go of his evil, he will be carried off with his evil.

We have on earth—and I can testify to this, since I travel the entire earth—hundreds of thousands of people (and we come in contact with tens of thousands of them) who are desirous of losing not only their diseases but their sins, their false appetites, their resentments, their jealousies, their envying, their malice, their lust, their greed. And because of Christ loosed in consciousness, they are finding healing.

Also, there are those in all parts of the world who still believe that it is perfectly all right to live by the sword. They do not know that in this age, they are going to hit up against the Christ and die by the sword. They do not realize that the weapon that they use against humanity is the weapon that will cut them down, and not in the far future but in the very near present.

As we have already noted, there was a time when man's inhumanity to man could make men rich and powerful; but that time has passed, that time is gone. There is a sufficient amount of the Christ loosed in human consciousness, that as evil hits up against that Christ, the evil is destroyed and the individual is set free. Again: only where the individual is determined to cling to the evil and benefit by it is the individual destroyed, along with the evil.

We are in that age, and, as we have also noted, we are in the age when children are being born into a world in which there is this greater measure of Christ. It will only be just another generation until there is so much Christ in the human consciousness that you will witness it. You will witness the Kingdom of God established on earth. That means there will be no more nights. There will be no more sin, no more disease, no more death. We will all be like the people in that mountain region of India who live to 120 or 140, then just fall asleep at night and go on to their transition.

Each one of us in turn makes the transition from visibility into invisibility and there is a good and natural reason for it. As long as we have a mission to perform in the visible, we will be here in the visible, but when that mission is accomplished, we will pass from the visible to the invisible, and we will continue to live—but on a higher spiral of spiritual life.

I would like to illustrate that for you so that you will no longer just believe in immortality but actually experience it. I will ask you for a moment to visualize, in your mind, a tree. I don't care what kind of tree it is, or where; however, somewhere on that tree are seeds. Now the life that is the life of the tree is the life of each seed. When that seed falls, or is carried somewhere and falls to earth, it sinks into the ground. The life of the tree is the life of the seed; therefore when that seed becomes a tree, it is that life that was a tree. In turn, that life which is the life of the seed is the life of the next tree. However, remember that it is the same life that was the life of the first tree.

Go back now in your mind until this is very clear to you. The life of the tree is the same life of the seed; therefore this same life is the life of tree number two, which is the life of the next seed, which in turn is the same life of tree number three. We have three trees—but we have only one life. Recalling that when you stand in front of a mirror, you cannot see yourself—you can only see your body— so, when you look at a tree, you cannot see the life, you can only see the body of the tree. The life is the invisible self, the invisible force or being. The tree is merely a form, just as what you see in the mirror is merely a form, a body. It isn't you.

You are that which is described in the word *I*. *I* is not a body; *I* is me. *I* is that which constitutes me. *I* is really my life, the life of me. Therefore as this body drops off, *I* do not drop off, for *I* am life. As a matter of fact, *I* am the life of this body. *I* am the life that gives this body its life, its direction. *I* am the life of this body, and as this body drops away, *I*, which is the life, immediately takes on a new body. I may look at it; it may be very strange to me at first, because I have witnessed that I can be male or I can be female. However, *I* am neither male nor female. *I* am incorporeal, spiritual life. It is only the body that has sex, not *I*.

So as you step forth from this body, you may at first find yourself in a strange place, looking at a body that is a bit strange to you. However, you will soon recognize that I am *I*, that you are you, and you will get used to the fact that you have a different body to function in and through. This body that you will have will be suitable to the atmosphere in which you are functioning. If you function on earth again, it will probably be a body similar to this one.

The more you realize that the life of a tree is immortal, that the life of the tree in your garden is the very life of the seed, and the life of the next tree, the more you realize your immortality. The more you realize your immortality, the more you realize my immortality—but that's not important. What *is* important is that you will immediately recognize that the life of your child, and the life of your grandchild, is immortal. Even before your child is born, long before your grandchild is born, you will be carrying around in consciousness the truth of the immortality and spiritual nature of the life of this unborn child, and this child then will be born into immortality.

Do you not see that *ye shall know the Truth, and the Truth shall set you free*? But it is only as you know the Truth about yourself. "O man, know thy self and you will know God." So says the Greek. Know thy self. Know thy self to be spirit, to be life, to be immortality. Then you will be knowing that for all of us, and you will be knowing it for the generation now being born. You will enable them to be born not into the mortality of threescore years and ten, more or less. You will be knowing them to be born into immortality, eternal life!

Then you will begin to understand the message that Christ Jesus gave to this world which has never been accepted, never at any time. That message comes with the realization of this passage that He also gave the world: *"I am come that you might have life and that you might have life more abundantly."* Repeat it to yourself: *"I* am come that you might have life and that you might have life more abundantly."

"I am come": do you see? That *I,* in the midst of you, is the He that is come so that you might have life and that you might have life more abundantly!

Therefore when I say, *"I,* Joel," or you say, *"I,* [your name]," just remember, that *I* has come into the midst of you *as* you so that you might have life—life more abundantly; in fact, life eternal. *I* am life eternal; *I.* Think now of the tree: the life of the tree is the life of the seed, which is the life of the next tree, which is the life of the next seed, which is the life of the next tree—and always it is that same life!

So you see that *I* am life. *I* am not the body. *I* am life and *I* am life eternal. Whether I am in the visible or whether my time has come to pass into the invisible is of no importance. *I* am life eternal.

Now if *I* am life eternal, if *I* am life immortal, if *I* am life spiritual, then that life of me is the Christ life, or the Presence of Christ. In the moment that you acknowledge that Christ, the Son of God, is your life, you have loosed more of the Christ into human consciousness. You have made sure that sin, disease, and death are thereby lessened, that the days of man's inhumanity to man are passing into the past, that the days of living by the sword, the taking up of weapons, are passing into the past.

In the recognition of the Christ of your being, you now have Christ on earth instead of mortal man. Of course, it would be impossible for you to believe for a moment that Christ is your identity without the prior realization that since God is my Father and your Father, Christ is universal identity.

If ten righteous—that is, spiritually enlightened—men can save a city, think what four hundred can do going out into the world, acknowledging, "Christ liveth my life, and those who touch my life touch Christ." Their sins, their diseases, their lacks and limitations are dissolved, not by virtue of me, but by virtue of *I* and my Father being one.

Anyone who touches my life, my consciousness—anyone who comes within my orbit—is lifted up spiritually. Their sins, their diseases, their false appetites, their lacks are lessened and destroyed. Those who insist on clinging to the sword are going to be destroyed along with it; and I am sorry, but we can't have any regrets about it.

This is why I know, since it was revealed within, that we are witnessing the ushering in of the second coming of the Christ. This means the coming of Christ to human consciousness, universally—not merely to the saints and sages, not merely to the few who become practitioners and teachers. Christ is now coming to earth as the consciousness of mankind.

You and I are ushering in that age in the recognition of the fact that *I* and my Father are one, that Christ is my individual consciousness and yours, and that everyone who touches me anywhere in this life's journey must automatically be lifted up, if only a grain higher, in spiritual consciousness—a grain less of sin, a grain less of disease, a grain less of old age, a grain less of false appetites. This must inevitably be. Then as you begin to realize Christ, you must consciously realize Christ as the identity of every individual. Now you are establishing the reign of Christ on earth.

You are part of that pioneer movement, and you don't have to belong to anything. You don't have to belong to any religion; God has no religion. God has no church; *you* are the Temple of God. Every individual is the Temple of God. There is no reason why you shouldn't belong to a church if you would like to, but belonging to it or not belonging to it has nothing to do with your relationship with God.

Your relationship with God has to do with an activity of your own consciousness, in which you realize that *I* and the Father are one. *I* am the Temple of God. *I* am the heir of God, joint heir to all the heavenly riches—to the Omniscience, the all-wisdom of God; to the Omnipresence of God; to the Omnipotence of God. *I* and my Father are one. This is a universal Truth.

We are all of the household of God. In acknowledging this for yourself, in bringing to yourself the harmonies that automatically follow the reign of Christ, do not forget that you are bringing them to this entire world. This is because in the last analysis we cannot wait for billions of people to decide to turn to Truth for the world to be saved. Nearly all the billions will pass on before this happens, and we will have to start all over with the next generation; and then *those* billions will be passing on before we can reach them.

Therefore, let's stop trying to reach mankind, and instead let each one of us determine to reach our selves, raise up Christ in our selves, realize the Christ in each other, and thereby establish the reign of Christ on earth. Then the billions of people will automatically discover that they are God-governed. When that day comes, if you witness it, you will probably be surprised that they are not grateful for it. They won't be grateful, because they will not know out of what they were lifted.

We witness that in our work. It used to puzzle me many years ago in the healing of so-called mental cases how all of a sudden we would witness a beautiful healing and yet the shocking thing was that they weren't grateful. They never said a word of thanks. It would puzzle you to think of this wonderful demonstration—and no thanks. Then all of a sudden you would realize: Of course! They never knew they were mentally disturbed at all. They know themselves only as they are now.

So it may be with us in that day when we truly recognize our Christhood. I am afraid we are going to forget to be grateful. Certainly, the new generation that is born into Christhood will never be grateful, for they will never know what they were saved from.

In earlier discussing the nature of the experience that happens to Christian Science students, Unity students, New Thought students, and Infinite Way students when they hit a certain moment in their life and pass from being just a human being to an awareness of this spiritual identity, my purpose was that you should know that in the moment when this experience happens to them, they become a spiritual influence unto hundreds and hundreds, and then unto thousands. Remember that in any degree whatsoever that you have experience of spiritual uplift, from that moment on you have become a spiritual influence unto hundreds and unto thousands, and you are ensuring the coming of the day of Christ as the consciousness of mankind.

What separates the life of an individual living the

human experience of both good and evil, sickness and health, abundance and lack, sin and purity, happiness and unhappiness, from the individual of spiritual attainment—whose life is, on the whole, a continuity of harmony—is a matter of identification. But I hasten to add that regardless of how high you attain on the spiritual Path, it does not mean that you will be forever without some problem or another. Yet it is safe to say, from what we have seen, that most of your problems will be minor ones and easily resolved. However, occasionally there can be some very serious problems that come along even to the spiritual student, and that is because of universal world hypnotism.

In other words, the mere fact that we are living in a world of other people means we cannot close our eyes to the troubles and problems of our friends and families. And sometimes we cannot close our eyes to the troubles and problems of the world, so that we come under the hypnotism of world belief and at any stage of our spiritual experience may encounter a serious problem.

We have, however, one great benefit over the rest of the world: no matter how great the problem is—even if we face death—it is not too much for us, because we have come to the realization that life here and life there is still *life*. So it is just going to be a matter of making the adjustment to life on one plane or to life on another. We are not quite as bad off as most people, who are living in fear of every pain because they are going to die. And of course, when the world faces serious problems, it has no answer.

It is a terrible spot to be in to have to face serious problems and to realize there are no answers. That cannot happen to us, because we know there is always an answer. It is just a matter of our attaining that answer, and the right degree of spiritual realization *is* the answer. We have something to work towards because we know that

if we were facing the last hour of our life on earth, this
verdict could be completely reversed within that hour, just
by correct realization. No matter what trouble we are
in, if we just have a practitioner or teacher of sufficient
spiritual consciousness, we are going to be pulled through
almost anything and everything.

However, we are probably free of 80 percent of all the
world's problems on this Path. Most of the 20 percent that
might touch us, we meet quickly, and the little that we do
not, we will meet eventually. *All* of it we will meet eventually on this plane or the next.

So the attaining of this spiritual awareness hinges on
right identification, on whether or not you have perceived
that *I* is God and are able not to think outward from the
standpoint of being man, limitation, subject to other laws.

While we know that 500 B.C. or thereabout, Gautama,
the Buddha, had his revelation, we do not know too much
of the nature of that revelation, or how it was worded.
However, we do know that in the experience of Moses we
have the full and complete revelation. This we know.
Moses revealed it forever to the world: "I am that *I am.*"

In the ancient Hebrew, one of these words was *Iham*,
as we would spell it today. *Iham* = "out here." So "out
here" is a person voicing God. The two are not the same.
There is a person voicing God, a person knowing God, a
person thinking God—and that is the sense of separation
that brings all of the troubles into the world.

However, when this man, who is a shepherd, realizes,
"Oh no; I am *That*," all of a sudden that shepherd becomes the leader and liberator of the whole Hebrew nation and is endowed with sufficient spiritual power to take
them right out from under the nose of Pharaoh and lead
them to the Promised Land.

It is said that Moses could not take the Hebrews into

the Promised Land because of some fault of his own; but I can tell you that is in error. This I can say through revelation. It was not any fault or mistake of Moses. The reason he could not take the Hebrews into the Promised Land is that *nobody* can take you into the Promised Land. They can only lead you *up to* the Promised Land and reveal this Truth to you; and if you do not accept it, you cannot walk into the Promised Land.

Nobody is ever going to take you into the Promised Land as long as you think there is man and God. Nobody! They can *lead* you to the Promised Land by telling you and writing books for you; but it is you who must attain the realization, "Oh, *I am!*" Then you will walk right into the Promised Land, and you will be right smack in the middle of it. "Oh, *I am!*"

Now you see, there is no more separation between you and God. *I* and the Father, who have always been one, now have become *One* in realization. "I and the Father are *One*" is the relationship between God and man, *Oneness*. The *Life* of God is the *Life* of man. There are not two; there is just *One*.

God breathed *His Life* into man, not man's life; God breathed *God's Life* into man. Therefore the *Life* of man *Is God*. God did not give man a mind; the *Mind of God* becomes the *Mind* of man, and it is for this reason that you can reach back and receive impartations from within yourself of a spiritual nature. If you are interested in the spiritual things of life, you can bring forth telephones, radios, televisions, cars, and planes, and all the things that have yet not been devised—because they are embodied in your consciousness. They were always embodied in Christopher Columbus, in Edison, in Ford, in Michelangelo, in da Vinci. They have always been embodied in the consciousness of man.

An artist, if he is a real artist, does not go to art galleries to look at pictures and then go home and paint. A musician who is a real composer does not go around listening to all the other composers' music and then go home and compose. The artist, the composer, the writer, goes within his consciousness and brings forth his art, his music, his literature. Why? Because his consciousness is infinite, because God constitutes his consciousness. Therefore by closing his eyes and going within, he is going to God.

The Master revealed this when He said, *"The Kingdom of God is neither lo here, nor lo there."* It is not up there in the holy mountain, it is not even there in the holy temple in Jerusalem. The Kingdom of God is within you! But what does the world do? It continues to look for holy mountains and holy temples and holy teachers instead of accepting what Moses revealed, Elijah revealed, Isaiah revealed, Jesus revealed, Paul revealed, John revealed, the Buddha revealed—and how many others I cannot even tell you, it has been known to so many. However, it has been lost always; to sum it up, you could say it was lost because it was organized.

The moment it was organized, we set up the Buddha, we set up Moses, and we set up Jesus. Always we set up someone, and they became the holy one, and we became the ones who sat at their feet and worshiped. They never taught this, they never encouraged it—never! No mystics in the history of the world have ever encouraged anyone to worship them. Sit at their feet to learn? Certainly: Accept this revelation and then *"Go, thou, and do likewise."* Whenever you found one who did not take that position, he was not a true mystic. It was someone who had some desire to be great or famous or rich.

The secret is "what I am, thou art; all that I am, thou art. All that I have is thine." Even God reveals that. So that you do not make the mistake of pleading with God for something, He even says, *"All that I have is thine."* How, then, after that can you pray for anything? *"All that I am, thou art."* How can you look to God for anything? The secret becomes knowing this Truth, living in this Truth, abiding in this Word, *"I am."* "All that God is, *I am*. All that the Father hath is Mine!"

CHAPTER 14

God's Grace Is Yours

A BIDE IN this Word, *"I am; all that God is, I am; and all that the Father hath is mine."* Then you will understand all of the Infinite Way writings, because they repeat over and over the Master's words *"I have meat the world knows not of. I have hidden manna. I will never leave me nor forsake me. I was with me before the world began. I will be with me unto the end of the world."* Whatever it is that I even think that I need or want, I have only to go within my own being. If I am just still and patient, the assurance will come, *"Be not afraid; it is I. I am thy bread, thy meat, thy wine, thy water. I will never leave thee nor forsake thee."*

It always comes from within. It always has come from within. Ever since my first spiritual experience, that has been my mode of life. Every time that I seem to be separated from any sense of good or any form of good, I have only to go within for the realization, and the assurance is given me. *"I go before thee to make the crooked places straight."*

As you read the writings of The Infinite Way, you will

see that the secret of The Infinite Way is in the word *I*.
That is the secret! Even if you go back to my basic textbook, which is the very first book of all, *The Infinite Way*,
you will see that it is founded on God appearing as man.
It is not God *and* man, not man going to God. The whole
of *The Infinite Way* is the revelation that God appears as
man. Then all that God Is, I Am; all that the Father has
Is mine. So the secret lies in going within to that *I* which
I Am!

You see, you do not know Joel at all. You are so far
from knowing Joel that if you really do come to find out
some day, you will be shocked at how little you ever knew
him. You do not know him at all! Joel does not even know
himself yet fully, and the reason is, I am Joel, and I have
not yet solved the full secret of *I*. When I find the full
secret of *I*, I will have the full name and identity of Joel.
However, what has made The Infinite Way a worldwide
activity, and so widely enjoyed and accepted, is the fact
that it is revealing *I*.

The Infinite Way is not only revealing *I* as the identity
of Joel. If it were, it would have a large following of non-
thinkers and idol-worshipers. But it does not have that
kind of followers, the reason being that Joel is glorifying
himself as *I*, but he is also telling you with every breath
in his body that this is also the Truth about you! Wake
up! Wake up! You are *I*, *I* is you, and infinity is the nature and the extent of your consciousness—this consciousness that is God. God Is your consciousness. Turn within!

Joel did not invent this; it is a rediscovery. Every true
mystic has known it, and some have been able to pass it
on to one or two, as Lao-tse did—just to one or two. I do
not know that Jesus was able to pass it on to anyone,
really—even to his disciples. Eventually Saul of Tarsus did
catch it from the Master, and Saul became Paul. Even-

tually, he who composed the manuscript that is now the Gospel of John also caught it from the Master. Whether or not any one of the Master's disciples caught it we have no record. There is no record that any one of them caught it.

All these other mystics usually found one, or two, or three who did. Gautama found several, but unfortunately those who did not catch it were the ones who took over, while those who did catch it, seeing the hopelessness of it, just wandered off by themselves. That may have happened in the Master's time, too.

The whole secret of harmonious living is embodied in the word *I*, and when you realize that *I* Is God, it is the only name you can use for God. There are no synonyms for God. Those that are called synonyms for God are not that at all; they merely describe attributes of God. When you say, "God is love," love is not a synonym for God, because there is not a synonym for the fullness of God. Love is merely one of the attributes of God.

When you say that God is mind or intelligence, it is not true. Mind or intelligence is an attribute of God. So it is when you say, "God is Spirit": that is not entirely true, because spirit is actually the substance of God, or consciousness is the substance of God.

The only time you are really declaring God is when you say *I*. This is the only word in any language that declares God. In fact, when you read in the Bible about "the Word," spelled with a capital W, the Word is *I*. When you are told to live in *My Word*, the Word to live in is *I*, and the way to live in it is to recognize *I and the Father are One*, not two.

God the Father is also God the son. When you try to separate God the Father and God the son, that is when you have a religion that cannot work. On the other hand, the moment you have one individual who claims to be God the Father and God the son, you have a religion that *can* work, because God the Father is God the son of every individual on the face of the globe, saint or sinner.

"*I* and the Father are One" is a spiritual relationship that was established in the beginning, before Abraham was. From the beginning, *I* and the Father have coexisted. *I* have lived in the bosom of the Father from the beginning, and even when *I* went forth to walk on earth, *I* never left the bosom of the Father, because *I* and the Father are inseparable and indivisible. The Master so recognized this that He was enabled to say, which heaven forbid any of us should say out loud today, *"Thou seest me, thou seest the Father that sent me."* Now remember, this is the Truth —but do not ever voice it, or there will be a man in a white jacket running after you.

"Thou seest me, thou seest the Father that sent me; for I and the Father are One, and all that the Father Is, I am; and all that the Father hath is mine." Therefore, since I know that God is spirit, then I know that all that the Father hath must be spiritual. So I do not go to the Father for loaves and fishes. I do not go to the Father for houses, automobiles, or employment.

That was a metaphysical blunder that delayed this revelation taking over mankind, because it never has been true that you can go to God for loaves and fishes. It never has been true that you can go to God for houses, automobiles, and parking spaces. That has never been true. God is Spirit, and you must worship God in Spirit and in Truth.

Therefore when you go to God, go to God for what we might call the gifts of God, the Grace of God. You might ask, "What are these?" and the answer would be, let us not worry about what these are, let us not be concerned. Just let us go for God's Grace. Turn within, because the

Kingdom of God Is within you; the *I* of you Is God. Turn within to this *I* for Thy Grace, for Thy Peace.

The Master says, *"My Peace give I unto thee, not as the world giveth."* Do not forget that! That is on almost every page of the Infinite Way writings. *"My Peace"* is not the peace that the world gives. Those who only want the world's peace had better stay away from God and find their own way of getting it. However, I do want the peace that God can give. Then I am no longer dependent on man, whose breath is in his nostrils; nor am I at the mercy of man, whose breath is in his nostrils—not the moment that I turn within for God's Grace, God's Peace, so that the Spirit of God may be upon me. This too the Master revealed: when the Spirit of God is upon you, you are ordained—ordained to be the spiritual son!

Do not forget that in your humanhood you are not the child of God. In your humanhood, I is not God, or we would all be individual Gods walking around, and none of us would ever be in trouble. In our humanhood we are the "natural man" that Paul revealed "is not of God, knoweth not the things of God, receiveth not the things of God, is not under the Law of God." That is what is wrong with this whole human race.

The human race can go to church and pray from now until doomsday; and if it is not careful, the roof of the church will fall on it. The "natural man" is not under the Law of God. That is why he can sin and have sinful appetites. That is why he can be diseased; that is why he can be uncharitable, unmerciful. There is nothing Godlike about him. He is an animal—virtually a beast.

When, however, an individual in one way or another is led to seeking, this means that something within him is trying to break through, because nobody of his own accord seeks God. You can put that down as a rule with no exception. No human being has of himself ever sought God—never in the history of the world! God has to seek you before you can turn and believe that you are seeking God. All the time that you are believing that you are seeking God, do not fool yourself; you are not! It is God in you that is trying to push through and reveal Himself to you. When you know this, you can stop your search for God and sit down and listen more, and then God will break through.

A human might seek happiness, and he might seek prosperity, and he might seek success, and he might seek fame, but it is not given to any human being to seek God. When you find anyone seeking God, you can be assured God started the search. God started it all by trying to break through. Then as we become aware of a hungering or thirsting, it is not really us—it is God starting to push through. And because we have not yet become aware, there is still that sense of separation.

The completion of our search for God never ends until —whether you receive the Message, whether you are spoken to, or whether it is just an inner experience—all of a sudden it dawns upon you: *"I and the Father are One,"* or *"I Am thou,"* or *"I will never leave thee nor forsake thee."* The moment that *I* voices Itself in there, you know that *I* is not man—*I* is God. Now you relax and rest in that *I* that I am. Now you do not have to take thought for your life, what you shall eat or what you shall drink, or wherewithal you shall be clothed. Now you rest, and life begins to be lived out from within yourself.

Then it is that you find you are a benediction to all who come within range of your thought. It is not because you are walking around blessing anybody but because, as you look at them, you are realizing that *I* at the center of their being, and you cannot help it. There, a smile comes to you when you stop to think. "*You* do not know it, but *I* know it. The Kingdom of God Is within you."

You would be surprised how many receptive people there are, how many people have a longing that awakens. You may never get to know them personally, you may never get to know whom you have blessed—although here and there you will find one who has said, "I find something," or "I feel something in you." What is it they feel in you? There is only one thing: your understanding of your identity and your understanding of their identity. That is what they feel! You are no longer looking at them with criticism, judgment, malice, hate, unforgiveness; you cannot anymore!

You can say, "I know what it is all about now: you thought you were man, you thought you were living your own experience. *Certainly*, if you did not seem to have money, you *had* to steal it or cheat or lie or make a false ad. If only you had chosen *I*, you would have realized— and without taking thought—that your own would come to you!"

Always remember that the only reason Burroughs could give the world that poem "Waiting" ("my own shall come to me") was because he had attained this. As a human being, no one can ever say, "My own shall come to me." As a human being, you know you have to go out and fight for it, advertise for it, struggle for it, labor for it. It is only when spiritual realization comes to you that you can say, "I can go and sit by the side of a stream and my own shall come to me." It will find you, wherever you may be; your employment, your art—whatever it is that is required to fulfill your life.

Here you must remember something. *I* Is God, but *I* appears as every individual, *individually*, as much so as fingerprints. In other words, no two of us are supposed to be the same. No two of us are required to do the same work. No two of us are supposed to express art, literature, music, or salesmanship in the same way. Each one of us has an individual gift. A thousand of us may play the piano or violin, but if we have made contact with our Center, each one will play it in an individual way. So it will not sound the same hearing Hofmann and hearing Paderewski. It will sound entirely different when you hear the two men at the same instrument.

So it will be in a painter, a sculptor, an architect. These days some might say, "Well, you can't include architects, because they only know one thing: square boxes with lots of glass"; but that is not true. That is only because circumstances have brought that about today; but the day will come when not one of these buildings will stand in the land, not one. They will all be pulled down, because the architect nature, the God-nature that is in certain individuals that makes them sculptors, artists, architects, will come to the fore and they will have to express in individual forms of beauty, art, and literature. However, this can only come about when we as individuals begin to understand that *I*, in the midst of me, Am mighty; *I*, in the midst of me, Am infinite; *I*, in the midst of me, Is God.

Now this Joel selfhood, which has not fully attained that realization, turns within—not to somebody else, but to the *I*, to the Center, to the Consciousness. Then forth from this Consciousness comes whatever it is that is necessary to my individual unfoldment, which may not at all be your individual unfoldment. You have to go within to the Center of your being, to the Consciousness of your being, and draw forth that which represents the fulfillment of your individuality.

This is why I think back very often to the ancient Hebrew prophets. People thought they were something set apart and great because they could prophesy. I will tell you the Truth: there was nothing unusual about it, nothing unusual at all! It is the easiest thing in the world to prophesy —and you will never make a mistake. Never! It is not wise to do it for the public because if you tell them something about next year that they do not already believe, they will crucify you for it. So, it is best not to prophesy in public. But it is easy to prophesy, and I will tell you why.

As you have these spiritual unfoldments, you will come to realize that the only permanent thing in the world is whatever it is that conforms to a Law of God. This is the only thing that eventually is going to be the permanent status of man. So when you see a teaching like socialism or communism, it is doomed! Why? It takes away from man his freedom and his individuality; instead he must be a part of a mass, he must be part of a herd, he must stand in line to collect his income.

That cannot last because the *I* is crying for escape. Not only the Hebrews under Pharaoh cried out for freedom; the Russians under the Czars cried out for freedom. The English cried out for freedom until they got their Magna Carta. The French cried out for freedom—until the guillotines were erected.

Do not ever hesitate to prophesy that the end of socialism and the end of communism is in sight, because man is crying inside of himself for freedom—because man is not man; God Is man; and God is not going to stay locked up in you forever! God is not going to stay locked up in a trade union that tells you how much you can earn when you cannot earn it. No! All of these things are doomed.

If you go back to the Hebrew prophets, you will find that the only thing they prophesied is that those of you who are living in limitation or holding others in bondage are going to be destroyed, and those of you who are seeking freedom are going to attain it. That is all they ever prophesied. All the prophets of doom prophesied the doom of those who were kings, those who were tyrants, those who limited. It is just as easy to prophesy that today.

God Is the mind of man, and the mind of man will not be limited or restricted or held in bondage—and do not think that it ever will. It will break through! There have been countries, as in the days of Pharaoh and even in modern days, that prevented their people from receiving education, and do you know that the very people responsible for that did not know why? They themselves could not tell you why—and there is only one reason: you cannot hold an educated man a slave and you cannot hold an educated man in bondage! The moment a man begins to know, he begins to Be, and you cannot hold him any longer.

Because the *I* of man Is God, start right now to be a prophet and prophesy that the ultimate fate of man is freedom. He does not have to bring it about by wars. He does not have to bring it about by rebellion. Gandhi saw that. Sit still and know *I* am God. Be still and know *I* am God. Pretty soon, those out there will begin setting you free, and they will not know why. Yes, you can prophesy that the fate of this world is freedom from sin, from disease, from death, from bondage, from limitation—and the beginning of that freedom comes with the realization of the nature of *I*. *Resist not evil,* just *Be still and know that I am God.* That is enough!

That one Truth will begin to break all of the crusts of limitation and outside powers that bind you. Just be still. Be still and know that *I* am God. *I* will never leave thee. *I* am thy bread, *I* am thy intelligence, *I* am thy safety, *I* am thy security. Live in the Word *"I."* However, be very careful! It has always been lost by revealing it to the unprepared thought—always!

This made people believe that they humanly were powerful. "Oh, I am God!" and then they began to be God, and they only destroyed themselves. I can tell you of movements that have existed down through the ages, broken up, and started again. Every time some group learned this secret that was not ready for it, they thought that it meant personal powers, or that it could make them a power over you, or make you a power over your nation. It is not meant that way. You do become a power unto everybody—but a power of Spirit, a power of Love, a power of Liberty; not a power over the private life of anyone.

Be still! Be still and know that *I* Am God. It is on this point that secrecy must become the absolute law with you. If you reveal it, you will lose it; and you will be sorry, because you probably will not regain it in this entire lifetime on earth. It has never been known that anyone lost it and regained it—not in any one lifetime. There have been people in past times who learned this and lost it. No history exists of anyone who ever regained it.

Therefore we do not reveal it. We may teach it, we may impart it as Jesus did with His disciples, as Gautama the Buddha did with his disciples—because we are not really violating secrecy. We have really become One consciousness, One mind, One life. We have really become a Body in which my interests are yours and yours are mine, and our interests are not personal; they are worldwide.

I do not live for myself. Pretty soon, you are going to discover that you cannot live for yourself. You cannot know this secret and just live a personal life for yourself. To some extent, your life will have to be dedicated. However, do not let it be dedicated to telling this to anyone until, in the course of time, you find students and become convinced that they are not sitting there looking for loaves and fishes or looking how to rule the world, but instead are looking how to be a greater dedication to the world than they already are. That is when you can gently—very gently—lead up to it.

If you will read the Infinite Way books again, you will see how gently it is led up to in every one of the books. Then you will say, "Why, Joel! I thought you were telling us something new out here! Why, you have already said this in every one of the books!" Yes, but many of you have not seen it there. When you go back, you will discover it there, but you will see that it has been touched on so gently, so lightly, that only those who have eyes to see will see it, only those who have ears to hear will hear it.

That leads up to this: from now on, normally and naturally, you should have more spiritual experiences than you have ever had in your life. If you have none, you *should* begin to have them—because all of our work is now at that stage. However, keep those experiences within yourself; do not share them with anyone. With your teacher, yes; your practitioner, yes; but not your husband or wife or friend or relative. This is because when you are having those experiences, no one but your teacher is at your state of unfoldment, and therefore no one else is going to be able to understand them. Keep them within yourself. Let them multiply, let them deepen, let them become enriched. Never fear them—although some of them come in a form that sometimes frightens. Anything that we are unfamiliar with can frighten us.

The student with whom I first meditated, after I'd had my own experiences in meditation, had felt she wanted to go far. One day we came to a place where, evidently, she was about to have an experience. It took the form of her feeling that she was falling down all the way from the sky to the earth. She got frightened and she screamed and she opened her eyes and said "Stop!" She was afraid of falling. She has never had a spiritual experience since, and she has never accomplished a meditation—and this was more than twenty-five years ago. Never has since! The fear, I suppose, keeps coming back. "Supposing I do fall?" I do not know where you are going to fall from or to, since you live and move and have your being in God.

Others have physical experiences. I went through that phase when it seemed as if the whole stomach was going to vibrate, over and over again. Sometimes even my heart was being pulled up and down, like a physical experience, and I would just look down and watch it. However, I have known others to have an experience like that and they became afraid of it. There is nothing to be afraid of if we are in God, and if God Is revealing Himself! That is nothing to be afraid of!

CHAPTER 15

A Great Secret

IF GOD is revealing Himself, there is nothing to be afraid of! Sometimes, if you read stories of Initiations—spiritual Initiations—you will discover that in these Initiations you have to go through terrible experiences. That is true; you do; but the thing is to make up your mind that this is the way it is going to be. Be a beholder and go through, because as long as it is a God-experience, the only reason it appears to be a terrible experience is that it is unknown to the human mind, it is unknown to us. It is not like anything we expected, therefore we think it is terrible. It is not terrible when it is finished, if we can stand long enough to go through.

Secrecy in spiritual matters is likened to the womb. The seed is planted in the womb and if it is not kept there, dark and secret, sacred, and fed within, it never will become the being—never! Secrecy is the womb of the spiritual life— that is where we take every experience: right into the womb of secrecy and sacredness. It must be sacred.

Another one of the evils of the human world is that it looks on human conception and birth as if it were something human—and sometimes even evil or sinful—and at best, physical. Now you see, this misses the whole point, because it is not so. It is something sacred; it is another individualization of God appearing. That is what it is; and in that light, it is not a human being that is born, and it is not the product of a carnal act that is taking place: it is *I* and the Father becoming One; and out of that Oneness is coming another One.

When our young couples, through spiritual study, realize this and realize that conception is not a carnal act, not something to be afraid of, or ashamed of, or something that is merely an act of pleasure—that actually it is a part of the nature of Living—then we shall discover that the seed is something sacred, not vulgar. It will be buried in the womb, and it will be held there secretly and sacredly as if we were waiting for God to appear, Christ incarnate. We *are* waiting for Christ to appear, the son of God to appear. When our youngsters wait with the understanding that they are waiting for the incarnation of Christ to appear, parentage will be something sacred, children will be something sacred, and we will begin living spiritually on earth.

A lot of people would like to convince us that, if we are spiritual, there will be no sexual relationships. However, if that is so, then we will be so spiritual that we will not have to eat, either, or drink water—and I do not believe that we are going to reach that for a while. I *do* believe that our spiritual life, for a long time to come, is going to be lived on earth, and that the method of this progressive life will be as it is now—only, instead of being accepted as just a human act, it is going to be understood as God's way of revealing Himself, or His Son, on earth. It is God's way of expressing Christhood on earth. Then the whole of this life is going to be as sacred.

Just remember that all over this world, where The Infinite Way has been meeting for many years, every one of our groups has been sacred. Our whole lives have been sacred, our whole relationship has been sacred, so why cannot the rest of the world carry that out too? They will the moment they know that *I* Is God!

To those of you who have been students of The Infinite Way for a very long time, many of you active in the practice, the healing work, and some of you at least starting it, I must bring to your attention the fact that you are engaged in a work that must inevitably set you apart from the rest of the people of the world—it either will or you will not get too far in your spiritual development. This is because you are not engaged in the study of a teaching so much as you are beginning to attain the fruitage of your search for Truth.

If you think back a few years in your experience, try to remember what it was that brought you into this particular message of The Infinite Way—whether it was primarily for a healing or some other aspect of better humanhood, or whether it was an actual desire, a search, or a reaching out for Reality, for Truth, for God. If, when you came into the work, your main idea was healing or human improvement, then whether or not your attitude has since changed, you should realize by now that merely improving your health or the amount of your supply is insignificant in comparison with the idea of actually finding the secret of life that is behind the appearance—behind what you see, hear, taste, touch, and smell.

You have realized by now that there is a great secret behind this world. It is a secret unknown to any of the religions, unknown to any of the philosophies, unknown to any "man, whose breath is in his nostrils." It is a secret of life that no man can know with his mind. It would make no difference what he studies, or where he goes to study, this secret he will never discover. That is why so few have entered in.

In the ages up to the present, most people have sought —and have expected of religions—human betterment and probably a promise of something great after they die. This is because the future is feared by most people—I mean the time beyond this immediate life, what is called "after death." Most people look to that experience with horror, with fear, with dread—and with good reason: most of the religions have presented that period as a period of getting the punishments that you did not receive here on earth, and with the vague hope that at some far distant time there might be heaven. Even heaven as it is described would be, if you attained it, a hell. By now, you must have discovered that there is nothing more monotonous than sitting and playing a harp all day and being happy.

However, the teachings of the world have not gone beyond seeking Truth through the mind, seeking Truth through books, seeking Truth through teachings—and of course, until you arrive at that place in consciousness where you realize that you never are going to find the Truth this way, you have not even begun your spiritual journey.

Your journey begins only when you come to the realization that going on as you have been going means you are never going to learn the Truth, this secret behind the universe, because it is not to be known with the mind or through the mind. While it is true that you do not know what the word *Spirit* means, nevertheless God Is Spirit, and that in Itself means that God is something that you do not know or understand; and since you have been searching almost a lifetime, it must get to be discouraging.

It *is* discouraging, because inevitably that realization

does come: "I never am going to discover God or Spirit, and my search is frustrating. What do I have to look forward to?" When you reach that point, you may be starting on your spiritual journey, because you will have reached the place where you can say, "Speak, Lord, thy servant heareth," and mean it—really mean it. "If You do not speak and I do not hear what You say, there is going to be no answer." When you reach that place, it actually means that you have come to the end of faith and hope and belief that the human mind is ever going to reveal spiritual Truth to you.

In one of our classes many years ago we had that for a title: "Abandon Hope All Ye Who Enter Here." In other words, abandon hope of finding God, all you who enter this class, because in this class you will not find Him. In this message, you will not find Him. The reason is that the Kingdom of God Is within you!

Now at the point in consciousness where you are, you do know that God is not going to be revealed to you in my words. The only opportunity of God's being revealed to you in our relationship is in what my consciousness can impart and in what your consciousness can receive, independent of words and thoughts.

In other words, there must be a relationship between us that transcends words and thoughts. There must be a state of consciousness that can receive that which an attained spiritual consciousness can impart. The teacher can impart it without words and thoughts but as a rule will use the means of words and thoughts and then let the Spirit in between do the actual imparting—that is, carry the import of the message.

I am leading up to this for a reason. I knew, when *The Thunder of Silence* was published, that I could not expect many people in the world to understand it or grasp it—

not even our students. I did not expect it and I still do not expect it for many, many years to come. The reason is that from the very outset, the message it gives contradicts the entire teaching of Christianity. It is a complete contradiction of all that is to be found in Christianity because every Christian teaching is based on God's goodness to you and God's punishment to the sinner.

Perhaps you have lived long enough to find out that God has not been too good to you. Probably you have discovered that God does not really punish the bad sinners at all and they seem to go scot-free. Once in a while, one of the sinners gets caught up by the law and gets sent to jail—but God does not seem to have anything to do with that; rather, it is the police department. As a thinker, you must find this puzzling. You must be startled at realizing how many sweet, loving, wonderful, good, and charitable people there are in the world whom God is not rewarding. It must amaze you how many evil people there are in the world that not only the law has not reached yet, but even God has not put His finger on.

As a thinker, you must ponder this, you have to give time and effort and thought to it, and then wonder if maybe the churches' explanation is a valid one—that if you do not get punished here, don't worry, you'll get punished somewhere else. No one has ever come back to prove their point that there is a hell or a limbo or any other place where you get punished afterward. I do not even know that the spiritualists have ever had messages from the "other side" saying that there is a very hot fire anywhere to burn you up. I have not heard of any such messages.

So it is that the longer you seek the answer with your mind, the more frustrating this is going to be. If you do not have an answer to it, you may be assured that not only will your frustration in life continue, but the solution to life's problems will not be given you. It is for this reason that those who were present when the first unfoldment came through my lips witnessed the fact that what came through my lips was not anything that I had known even five minutes before.

It was something that came through and startled me as much as it did any of those who were listening and caught it. Be assured, I had to do a great deal of thinking and meditating after the Message came through in order to realize the astounding nature of what it was. I even said, afterward, "I hope there were no reporters present, because if that Message were reported in the papers, I am sure the churches would have done to me what they did to the ancient revelators." That day, the Message that came through said, *"God neither punishes nor rewards."* You search the literature of the world and see what a startling Message that is, how it refutes the religious teachings of most of the world, and of all the Western world.

Since God neither punishes nor rewards, and since, as we have found, there is a certain amount of punishment and reward that goes on in this world, what is the answer? The answer that came through was what the Hindus call karmic law, that which Jesus called, *"As ye sow, so shall ye reap."* Whether you quote the Orient or whether you quote Jesus, you throw all Christian teachings out the window, because if it is "As ye sow, so shall ye reap," then it has nothing to do with God on either the punishment side or the reward side. It has to do with the law that you set in motion. When we go to Brother Paul, we find him receiving that same revelation from the Christ: *"If you sow to the Spirit, you will reap life everlasting. If you sow to the flesh, you reap corruption."* So here we have it in the basic Christian teachings: "As ye sow, so shall ye reap"; and please leave God out of it!

Unfortunately, the basic Christian teaching was not incorporated into the Christian Church. It is for this reason that Dr. Jung was able to write that he never had a case of a person over thirty-five years of age who had been healed through his ministry without a return to basic religion. However, it was not the religion of the churches; nor had he ever had a failure of healing in a person over thirty-five years of age that could not be traced to the fact that they would not return to a basic religious teaching—but, he emphasized, not the teaching of the churches. Why did he make that distinction?

The teaching Dr. Jung gave to the world in his later years came to him through a revelation. The teaching in the earlier years came through his medical studies, but in the later years he had a spiritual revelation, and it was then that he discovered a return to basic religion. He said it could be any of the basic religious teachings, Oriental or Occidental, as long as you remained with the original teachings of the original Revelators! Here is one of the reasons why through revelation you learn the nature of God. Then you will discover, when you know the nature of God, that there is nothing in this nature that either punishes or rewards.

Let us, for a moment, think of God as Life—the Life of the universe, the Life of all nature, as well as our own lives. Since God Is from everlasting to everlasting, the nature of God must be eternity, infinity. There could be nothing in the nature of God that would shorten the life of man or the universe; therefore the life of man must be eternal and immortal. So right here you have *no punishment*—because all of our sins and diseases and deaths are supposed to be due to punishment. All our accidents, all the evils that befall us, are supposed to be due to punishment of one nature or another. "God's will" it is called—"God's will" that an airplane collapses with a hundred people on board, "God's will" that a steamship burns at sea or hits an iceberg. Do you not see that this was not in the original teaching of Jesus Christ?

Do you not see that if you go back to the Gospels, you cannot find that God destroys life for any reason, since Jesus' mission was to raise the dead, to do the works of God, to show forth eternal life? His mission was to heal the sick and even to forgive the sinners. So God could not have provided both a punishment for sinners and forgiveness at the same time.

Therefore if you go back to the basic teaching of Jesus Christ, you will discover that there is no punishment through God, no reward through God, and that it is "As you sow, so shall you reap." Of course, when you turn to the Oriental teachings where they have karma, you will also discover that it is your sowing that results in your reaping, and your reaping goes on until the sowing changes.

If you can catch solidly and firmly this revelation in *The Thunder of Silence* and actually bear witness to the fact or come to a conviction within yourself, and can leave God right out of your calculations, out of your thinking, as far as your rewards and punishments are concerned, or your health or sickness, or your life and death—see if you cannot grasp this principle that "As ye sow, so shall ye reap." Then make the acknowledgment, "Regardless of where I am in life, regardless of what experience I may now be having: somewhere or other there is a sowing in my consciousness that is responsible for a reaping," and see if you cannot find it.

If you can grasp this teaching of The Infinite Way, you are half way home—because if you are still seeking around in your mind hoping for a God to do something or change something, you are still back in orthodoxy, you are still waiting for that which is not going to happen. Whatever is going to happen, is going to happen as an activity of your consciousness!

Until you come to the full realization of the startling nature of what I am saying to you, it does not seem startling to you at all. The only reason it does not is that you have not grasped it. But when you reach that, the rest is going to be easy—because I will tell you a secret of something that is operating in the back of your consciousness— unnecessarily—and causing you distress: there is still a belief in your thought that some acts of commission or omission on your part are responsible for your discords or inharmonies.

Here again is where the Church has led you completely astray—because the Church is 100 percent in error in telling you that any sin of yours is responsible for the woes that you may have experienced, or may be experiencing, or think you ever may experience. Be assured it isn't that way at all. You just might as well forgive yourself right now and forget about your past sins or present ones of commission or omission. Drop out of your thought, right now, that it was any error of yours.

Remember, when I speak this way I am telling you what you must be holding in thought about your patients and students. Do not forget that I am not speaking primarily to you who already have come a great part of the way along this Path. I am reminding you of what you must be revealing to your patients and students in order to free them from their guilt complexes and from the belief that they should be expecting a reward for the good things they have done in life or a punishment for the bad things that they may have done or for the good things they left undone. You must set them free. You perhaps have been in great measure already set free by your studies and work; but I am giving this to you so that you may complete your demonstration, that you may have the full awareness of dealing with those who come to you.

What is the sowing and the reaping that is causing the distresses of the people on earth? Paul summed it up, and we will have to do what he probably did, which never got into print: we will have to explain it. Paul merely stated it (to those around him he may have explained it, but it was never printed): "If you sow to the Spirit, you will reap life everlasting; if you sow to the flesh, you will reap corruption." That is the statement, and the explanation is this: you were born into a material sense of life, therefore you have been sowing to the flesh all of your human life. You have put your entire hope, faith, and confidence into form and effect.

We have been brought up, naturally, to believe that money was supply, and it is this teaching that really causes all the lack and limitation on earth, because whether you believe that money or crops were supply, it is equally in error. Consciousness is supply, Spirit is supply, the Invisible is supply—That over which you have no control but That which can, when you permit It, control you, govern you, fulfill you.

To believe for a moment that money, investments, securities, jobs, professions, and businesses are supply—or just to be born into the belief that they are supply—makes you go out to get these and thereby cheats you of the demonstration of supply; because these are not supply. When you go far enough in the message of The Infinite Way, you will discover that *I* am supply, that *I* embody and embrace within me the infinity of supply—and not only for my own use. *I* could feed five thousand because *I* Is God.

Now, deny that *I* am supply! *I* am the bread, the meat, the wine, the water. *I* am the resurrection. *I* am life eternal. *I* can give you water; drinking it you will never thirst again. *I* am the bread of life. Until you actually accept that, you are going to be sowing to the flesh and you are going to reap limitation.

There are people that reap a million dollars' worth of limitation, ten million dollars' worth of limitation—but it *is* limitation. The proof of it is that after they get it, they sometimes cannot eat twenty-five cents' worth of food, and sometimes they cannot spend any of it. They have to sit and just watch it and count it and multiply it, and they can no more part with it than they can part with their blood. Do you see that? We all know that money, in and of itself, cannot spend itself. It takes the spirit of a man to part with it, to share it, to give it, to distribute it. The money itself will not do that!

Therefore just to be born into an ordinary family means to be born into limitation, into the struggle to earn a living, into strife—whereas in being born into a family of spiritual understanding, a child would be brought up right from the beginning to sow to the Spirit, realizing that love is supply, life is supply, God is supply, and *I* am supply. That child would grow up with such a different concept of supply that it would never work for it or struggle for it or lie for it or cheat for it. Whatever activity the child undertook—and do not forget some would be artists, some would be doctors, some would be lawyers, some would be designers and builders, and all the rest of this— they would be doing it for the joy of life, they would be doing it as a Gift of God, a Grace of God.

It really makes no difference what work you are doing

in life, the moment you are not doing it for a living, it becomes a joy. When you are doing it for a living, you cannot help watching the clock, wondering whether you are giving more than you are getting. The moment that you do not connect supply with your living, then your activity, your work, your art, your business, your profession becomes such a joy that you are giving yourself to it, you are sowing to the Spirit. Supply, then, may come through that avenue, and it may come through very many others.

CHAPTER 16

Sowing to the Flesh

HAVING BEEN born into an ordinary religious family, what really were the first words we heard? We did not hear them with our ears but they went into our consciousness. The first words we heard after we came out of our mother's womb were, "Be careful, do not drop the baby, do not get the baby in a draught." From that second on, you can be assured we were sowing to the flesh, we were watching the body, we were watching draughts, we were watching cold feet, we were watching germs. We were doing something that made us apprehensive about the body.

Always, the first thing a youngster learns when they go to school is, "Do not talk to strangers; it might be a kidnapper." There is only one kidnapper in a million people; but it might be a kidnapper. So a fear of kidnappers goes into every child, whereas only one in a million ever meets one. Do you see how we sow to the flesh instead of being taught from the beginning, "These people are your brothers and sisters, these are children of God." But no, they might be a kidnapper; and even if they are not, they do not belong to your church, and that makes it bad; they do not belong to your race or your religion, and that makes it bad; or they do not belong to your nation, and that makes it bad.

Do you not see what I mean by "Sowing to the flesh, you reap corruption"? It has nothing to do with your personal sins! Your personal sins and mine—never let me omit mine—are due to the fact that we were born into this sowing to the flesh. Therefore, this became a pleasure of the flesh, that became a pain to the flesh, this became desirable to the flesh, that became undesirable to the flesh —and all we have done is cater to the flesh.

Now what of the Spirit? Well who ever heard of that? Who ever heard of the invisible Spirit that is in us, which Is the Spirit of God in man? Who ever directed our attention to the Spirit of God in our neighbor or to the Spirit of God in the sinner? Who ever directed our attention to the fact that not only the saints but all sinners have the same Spirit of God in them, and only our ignorance of this Truth brings upon us the discords of the flesh, even the diseases?

If it was not so ingrained in us to fear weather, and fear climate, and fear germs, and fear infection, we really would not have half the things that are wrong with us. So it is not our personal sins—it is that which we have personally accepted of the universal belief, through our ignorance. Ignorance is our major sin. That is why, in one of the most joyous books I have ever read, some of our saints approach heaven and they are shocked to see some of the world's sinners up there and they want an explanation of it. So God has to say to them, "Sin? Sin? There is only one sin: ignorance. Anything else, you can come in here. We have thieves up here, we have adulterers up here, we have everything. There is only one sin and that is ignorance, and the ignorant cannot get in, even though they were saints on earth." Well, that is burlesque—but it is a burlesque of the Truth.

Only the ignorant remain out of heaven, or harmony. The sinners get into heaven because the moment they are enlightened, there is no more sin, and a person who is not sinning is not a sinner. Whatever happened yesterday, last week, last month, *"though your sins were scarlet, you are white as snow"* is in the basic Christian teaching—not in the Church's. You can still be excommunicated in the Church. If you were a sinner ten years ago, you may not be admitted today. However in basic Christianity, though your sins were scarlet, you are white as snow in that very moment when your ignorance is overcome and you begin to realize, "Any wrong that I have done of a major nature or a minor nature is based only on my ignorance." That is all! Had there already been enlightenment, it could never have happened. How do we know that?

Enlightened people do not do wrong. It is an impossibility for a spiritually enlightened person to do wrong. Why? Because there is nothing out there worth having enough to do wrong for. What is it out there that you want that badly when you have the Kingdom of God in here? You do not have to lie, cheat, steal, and defraud for supply, because the moment that you realize the nature of supply, it begins to flow, and that ends that.

Pleasures? Who has to cheat for pleasures when all the pleasure there is in the world is unfolding from within? If it takes two, the two will be provided. If it takes six, the six will be provided. No need to go out looking.

The Infinite Way is a startling revelation, a radical one. It goes back to absolute basic religion, the religion of Revelators in the days when there was neither good nor evil; that is, the revelations of the Revelators announced that there is neither good nor evil—only thinking makes it so. You would be surprised at what happens in your personal life when you come to an actual realization that there is nothing good or evil and that it is only habit, custom, belief, tradition that makes it so. Things that are right in one place are wrong in another place. Things that are moral in one place are immoral in another place.

I am thinking of states that have laws: a fifty-dollar fine if you are caught taking an orange off this orange tree, or a pineapple out of this pineapple field. Well, it is not wrong to take an orange off an orange tree or a pineapple off a pineapple field, no matter who the tree or the field belongs to. It is definitely not wrong! *"The earth is the Lord's and the fullness thereof. Son, all that I have is thine."* That is the only real Law there is. The other is a man-made law to protect what is not his, to make it seem that it is his, and then throw a fence around it.

Do you not see? Well, there was quite an article in the paper about it today. It said that with only 8 percent of our workers in the United States in agriculture, we are turning out not only more food than this nation can eat, but more than all the nations that are buying it can afford to pay—and still the storehouses are full—whereas in Russia, with nearly 50 percent of the people in agriculture, they do not have even enough for their own country.

The reason for our overabundance must be know-how: knowledge, understanding! The reason for their lack is lack of know-how. Then do you not see that it is not really God that has anything to do with our great abundance of crops as a reward for our virtues (God forgive), nor is it a punishment to Russia that they have not enough crops—that it is just a matter of sowing and reaping? Neither nation knows that if those nations that have overabundance were to share freely with those who have not, eventually it would make for all nations having an overabundance, and the situation in life would be different.

However, can that be while you are sowing to the flesh and believing, "I am rich while I have it in the storehouse, even though it may be rotting there"? No! Sowing to the flesh reaps corruption, because sometimes sowing to the flesh reaps an overabundance, and the overabundance corrupts the morals. It certainly corrodes the Soul. Can it help corroding the soul to know that we have an overabundance and somebody else is starving? Can it help hurting? Of course, it cannot. Therefore in our individual experience, when we are sowing to the Spirit, that cannot happen to us. We are not being corroded because freely we can give. We cannot give away the government's and we cannot give away our neighbor's, so we cannot prevent their demonstration. However, we need not sow to the flesh to the extent that we believe that we must hold back while others are lacking. We can be as free as our own spirit permits, thereby proving that we are sowing to the Spirit and not to the flesh.

This goes in another direction also. I am going to share with you part of a talk given by the President of West Germany on the Jewish feast of the New Year:

"Thirty years ago, Hitler brought about that power with his government that led our nation nearly to the abyss. Five years later, this government revealed its depravity and villainy by the persecution of our Jewish fellow-citizens. The suffering of the Jews under the Brown Government was a horrible witness of the degeneration of public power and civilization. The cause of all crimes and misdeeds that dishonored the German name was the ideology of inhumanity, hatred, and injustice. It would be useless to talk about the shadows of this terrible past with indignation and shame as expiation. Such days of remembrance remind us to overcome the past by thinking and acting in the spirit of confidence and charity.''

Now "though your sins were scarlet, you are white as snow"; and in a public declaration of that kind, the government gives voice to what actually has been happening among the people in the past few years: the realization of that horror, injustice, inhumanity, disgrace. In this personal and governmental acknowledgment, the karma is wiped out. *Though your sins were scarlet, you are white as snow.* Those persons of Germany who feel this way, as well as the government of Germany, are freed from punishment. It is not the punishment of God. God never punished them for any of their sins. The sowing had to bring forth reaping. Now with the sowing of a message of this nature, there is the reaping of what we call forgiveness, or release from punishment. Thereby a nation is set free.

If you do not understand this law of karma, you will not understand the reasons not only for the sufferings of many Americans individually, but for the horrors of our government—the discords and disharmonies that it is suffering, the lack of ability to arrive at a solution to any major problem. Unless you understand this law, you cannot even help, as a citizen, to bring forth harmony.

We individually, and the government as a government, must acknowledge guilt in antisemitism, in the Negro situation of the South and in parts of the North, in the Japanese persecution in California during the war, and last but not least, in the atomic bomb. Until you as an individual come to an inner agreement that destroying civilian populations by atomic bombs is inexcusable, you are under that karma, because *"resist not evil"* is the basic Christian teaching; *"lay down your life rather than take*

another life" is a basic Christian teaching; but certainly
"save your life at the expense of another's" never is.

We at this particular period have no right to interfere
with governments who have adopted warfare as a part of
natural Christian living. As long as warfare continues, you
may have to play your part in it; but to accept within your
consciousness the rightness of it brings you under "sowing to the flesh." If you believe that it is right to protect
your property or your life at the expense of someone else's
life, you are sowing to the flesh. If you believe that it is
right to destroy a civilian population to win a war, you are
sowing to the flesh and there is no way to experience anything other than that karma.

But you as an individual can come out from under this
and say, "I cannot lend my approval to that," within
yourself. Publicly you are not supposed to say anything,
because you are not called upon; you must inwardly come
to that place in consciousness where you cannot take
another person's life believing in the rightness of it. Then
you have come out from under that karma; but your nation still is not out until, through its government, it likewise voices its disapproval of racial persecution, religious
persecution, color persecution, persecution of any kind,
or the wanton destruction of civilian life in warfare.

You will not find God through the human mind. As you
work now with this understanding of karma, sowing and
reaping, remember that for enlightenment, you have to
open your consciousness to "Speak, Lord, Thy servant
heareth" and begin to receive spiritual impartations
through the new consciousness that you have developed.

We are seeing now the meaning of a way of life, a spiritual way of life, an Infinite Way of life, a mystical way
of life—and this way of life is the direct opposite of the

material way of life or even what we might call the human way of life. In this material or human way of life, I am acted upon. In other words, I may have a good experience because somebody is good to me, or I may have a bad experience because somebody is bad to me. I may have a healthy experience because the weather or the climate suits me, or I may have an unhealthy experience because the weather, or the climate, or the food does not agree with me.

I may be prosperous because I am in a prosperous country, or in a prosperous part of the country, or in a prosperous industry. I may not be prosperous because my particular industry is no longer prosperous, or because the part of the country where I live and have my business is having a recession, or even the whole country is having a recession. We may even have a war and part of our people begin to prosper and the other part of our people begin to get killed and wounded.

Now all this is the material or human way of life, in which we are acted upon and in which we do not govern or control, because somebody is always doing it for us— somebody or something.

In the spiritual way of life, you have the opposite of this. You are not at the mercy of "man, whose breath is in his nostrils," you are not under the control of people, circumstances, or conditions. On the contrary, you set the stage for your own experience. You are at all times in control of the situations that govern your experience.

I have described this elsewhere in its relationship to supply. Once you understand the spiritual way of life, it would be impossible to lack. It would be impossible because infinity is the measure of your supply. There isn't anyone that can give it to you and there isn't anyone that can take it from you. It is something that you set in motion yourself by attuning to the spiritual law of supply.

The first requirement is that you must know what the spiritual Law of supply is. You learn, either through meditation in which it is revealed to you, or from the experience of those who have discovered it and who present it to you. The secret of the Law of supply, spiritually, is in the passage "What have you in your house?" What *have* you now in your "house"? You begin to search your own consciousness for what you have at this moment, and then you begin to pour, as the poor widow poured the few drops of oil that she had and then found that the cruse did not run dry.

The moment you begin to pour out what you have in the house, or the moment you withdraw your attention from your usual means of supply, the outward source of supply, you begin to take your attention from that world and pour from your consciousness. "What have I in the house?" *house* meaning consciousness: "What have I in my consciousness?" *"I and my Father are One. Son, thou art ever with me; all that I have is thine."* Therefore I do have something in my consciousness, I do have something that has been given me of God; I do have, I do possess. What is it? What am I withholding? What am I holding back? What is it that I have that I am ignorant of? What is it that I am not pouring?

My consciousness is infinite because it is One with God. Because I am One with God, all that the Father hath is mine. I have infinity but I am not pouring forth all that I should. Somewhere, somehow, I am damming up my supply, I am holding back and not letting it flow. It has nothing to do with anyone outside of me: no one is giving to me and no one is withholding from me, because

God is the Source of my being, God is the Source of my supply—God is even the Measure of my supply. That is why my Measure is infinity itself.

I may find that I have some clothing that I can share, I may find that I have some food or some service. Then, of course, I realize that the greatest meaning in this whole experience of supply is spiritual. Have I become a Son of God? Because, if I have become a Son of God, then I am heir—joint heir—to all of the riches. But *have* I become a Son of God; or am I still that "natural man" that receiveth not the things of God? How do I know whether I am the Son of God?

Of course, the biggest guide I have is the teaching of Christ Jesus. Am I fulfilling the Law of Sonship? What is the Law of Sonship? According to the Master, it is that I pray for my enemies, that I pray for those who despitefully use me, that I forgive—seventy times seven—that I serve. *"Inasmuch as ye have done it unto the least of these my brethren, ye have done it unto me."* I must serve, I must help, not only my family, not only my friends, not only those of my own religious family. Impartially I must find a way not only to educate my children, but to help educate the children of those who cannot afford that education. I must clothe not only my children; I must find a way to help in the clothing of those children whose parents have not awakened yet to their true identity.

From me must pour forth supply! I must give it in the mundane things in life, and I must give it in the more spiritual things, the prayers. The prayers for the enemy, the forgiveness of those who offend. I must pray without ceasing. I must abide in the Word and let the Word abide in me. I must fulfill all that the Master reveals as constituting the Son of God, the Christ of God.

If I am to declare myself to be the Son of God, or the

Christ of God, I must act like it. I must not take the Name, I must not wear the Garment, and then not fulfill it. That is hypocrisy, that is spiritual wickedness in high places! If I call myself the Son of God, I must set aside my time for the practice of forgiveness, of praying for the enemy, of resisting not evil, of not taking up the sword, of not retaliating, of not using "an eye for an eye and a tooth for a tooth."

This is the beginning, then. If I know that the Law of supply is outgiving, outpouring, expressing, then I govern my own supply. It is not governed by what anyone wants to give me or by what anyone wants to withhold from me. It is governed purely by my own degree of givingness. Therefore no longer is supply a problem. The only problem is, am I sufficiently expressing my supply, letting supply flow through me? Therefore I am always "in the saddle" on the subject of supply. When I wish to increase it, I have to increase the measure, the degree, of my outflow of prayer, service, and so forth.

So it is, then, that my entire experience on the spiritual Path depends not on you in your relationship to me—by *you* I mean anyone in the world—but on my relationship to all of "you" out there in the world. My demonstration of harmony depends on what I am seeing out there. It does not depend on you. It does not depend on your attitude to me. It does not depend on whether you like me or believe me. It does not depend on whether you ever know me. It depends on my attitude to you. Either through spiritual revelation or through following the teaching of those who have had spiritual revelation, you come to know this.

The harmony of my life depends on my oneness with the Source of all Being and the obedience to Its Laws. It all has its foundation in this statement. *"Ye shall know*

the Truth, and the Truth shall make you free." Now, this
is the Truth; I am looking "out there" and seeing that you
are the Christ, or Son of God. You are spiritual! Remember, I am not saying what you should do; I am telling you
now what I must do if I would have harmony in my life.
You will find, sooner or later, that you must do it, too,
if you want harmony in your life.

I must acknowledge no man on earth to be my Father.
By doing this, I do away with my nationalism, I do away
with my religious fanaticism, bigotry, bias, prejudice—
because there is but one Father. This is the Truth: there
is but one Father, and this Father is Spirit, and we are the
offspring of Spirit—not of man. Man is not a Creator.
God is the Creative Principle of all life, God is the Source
of all life, God is the Principle of Life. Therefore God is
the only Father.

Since God is the only Father, we are brethren, we are
brothers and sisters. Like it or not, that is the Truth!
Whether we are Jew or Gentile, Protestant or Catholic,
white or black, Oriental or Occidental: like it or not, the
Truth is that there is but one Father, and this Father Is
Spirit; and we are the offspring of that Father!

Now in the moment that I make this agreement—that
God is your Father and my Father, that we are brothers
and sisters, that we are one spiritual Household—then
we are of the Family of God! Whether or not I say it in
words, the fact is that I now love you. I cannot help it: you
are all offspring of the same Parent that I have.

We are all one Family. This love is not a personal one
and it is not a sensual one; it is an absolutely spiritual
agreement that we are brothers and sisters and that we are
One. All that my Father hath is yours, the same as all that
my Father hath is mine—because it is the same Father
speaking to the same Son, which you are, which I am.

CHAPTER 17

The Power of Truth

WE ARE all brothers and sisters, we are One, and we are one Family. All that my Father hath is yours, the same as all that my Father hath is mine—because it is the same Father speaking to the same Son, which you are and which I am. The moment I see that this is your relationship, do you not realize there is a bond between us? I did not establish that bond nor did you. God established that bond. However, I recognize it and have brought myself into obedience to it and to oneness with it, and now this Law of the Fatherhood of God and the Brotherhood of man is in operation in my life.

By my perceiving this, not only my attitude to you changes, but your attitude to me changes. Remember, I am speaking of everyone in this world. So even when I go out into the world of strangers, into the hotels, into the airports, into the publishing market, into the business world or any other, just think what happens in my recognition that all these people are offspring of God—my brothers and my sisters. I have this feeling toward them, and can you not see what feeling must come back to me?

It is better than an insurance policy, I promise you; *much* better.

This is because the love that is poured out must come back. It has to; it's continuously like "bread cast upon the waters": it goes out, true, but the next tide brings it back. So it is that this love that is poured out—and you must see the nature of this love—is a love that is Truth, really. This Truth I am pouring out in the recognition of you as my brother or my sister, child of my Father. It compels me to treat you honorably. It compels me not to act towards you in any manner that I wouldn't act towards a member of my household. It compels me because you are of my household. The fact that we live under different roofs has nothing to do with it. Lots of my family live under different roofs. It doesn't change our relationship.

Now, this very love that I am pouring out, this very Truth of being, you can feel. The reason you can feel it is this: there Is only one Mind. Whatever Truth is taking place in my mind, you feel. That is how it is that you can have healing through a practitioner. Whatever Truth the practitioner knows, the patient responds to. The practitioner does not have to project his thought to a patient. That was the old-fashioned method of treatment, and it has no place anymore in spiritual work. As long as I know that I and the Father are One, and that I am at One with God, and all that the Father hath Is mine, anyone who has reached out to me for help receives the power of that Truth. Why? Because it took place in the one Mind.

We are not separate minds. There is only one Mind, and every bit of Truth that permeates my being is at the same moment permeating the being of all who are receptive. Therefore the love that I pour out is poured back to me. Let me show you a concrete illustration of this.

After a lesson of this nature, one of our students—a

girl—left the classroom and went home on a bus. On the bus there was a very intoxicated man, who was very boisterous and using unseemly language. This student sat quietly, realizing the essence of this lesson: that there is only One of us; that there is only one God, one Principle; that we are all of one Household, and so forth. This student found her Peace, and very soon this man quieted down. Then, when the man went to leave the bus, he stopped by this girl, touched her on the shoulder, and said, "Thank you for praying for me; I will never drink again."

Another experience involved a girl leaving the class one night, who went down to the coffee shop in the hotel and had a similar encounter, and acted in the same way. This man came up to her and said, "Would you please talk to me about God." So she talked to him about God for a half-hour. He left just as sober as a judge.

The point is, you see, that whatever of spiritual Truth there is operating in my consciousness is felt by you. This is because we are only One mind. We are together in One place, of One Mind. We are all in one Consciousness. More especially is this true when we come together.

Now my attitude towards this world is the attitude that the world pays back to me. I am not speaking of this in any human sense—that if I am a good man the world will be good to me. We've all seen how that does not work. We have all seen many times how good we have been to certain people and then found that knife right down our back to the hilt. There isn't any of us here who has not had that experience. So it would be folly to say to you that if you are good to others, they will be good to you. That is a dream that people have wakened up from with that knife.

No, I don't say be good to anyone and they'll be good to you. I am not saying that as you are to others, so they

will be to you. I am saying that the Truth that you know
is what will return to you, *this Truth that you know*.
If you know this Truth—that God is the only Father,
the only Cause and Creative Principle, and that we are
brothers and sisters—then this compels you to act towards
this world with justice, kindness, benevolence, integrity.

So you can be assured of this: the very Truth that I am
knowing about you, you respond to. It is the way in which
I am seeing, through knowing the Truth, that brings back
my experience. Let me show you this in another way. In
the human way of life, and as you may have been taught
in psychology, people are made up of good and evil. So
they do good and they do evil. Of course that isn't true.
It never was true. The only truth about it is, that is what
man has created in his dream. As long as man believes
that, that is what happens to him; "in accordance with
your faith, so will it be unto you." As long as you believe
that men are good and evil, or that some are good or some
are evil, or that they are all made up of some good and
some evil, that is exactly what is going to be measured
back to you. Your own belief is going to come back to
you.

You should awaken to this Truth, that there is no evil
in anyone. All evil is an activity of the carnal mind; it is
not of man. You must remember, we have already established who you are. Since there is only one Father, you are
the child of that Father. You are heir of God—joint heir.
You are the very Christ of God; we know now who you
are. Therefore any evil—sin, disease, death, lack, old age,
anything you want to call it—that appears to be in you I
recognize to be a delusion of the senses. It is an illusory
picture that is being presented to me by the carnal mind.
I am no more fooled by it than I am fooled by an ocean

in the middle of the desert, or by the sky that sits on the mountaintop but doesn't.

I am not fooled by appearances, because the Truth of your identity has been revealed to me. Therefore when sin, false appetite, disease, old age, death—any such appearance of discord—presents itself to me, I must know the Truth. God is not the author of sin, disease, or death. God is not in the whirlwind. God is not in the evils of the human world. God is in the still, small Voice that is in the midst of you. Therefore I stop malpracticing you!

Remember that *as a human being*, my whole life is devoted to malpracticing you. I am seeing you sick, or I am seeing you sinful, or I am seeing you old, or I am seeing you dying. That is mental malpractice—nothing more, nothing less. Every one of us is guilty of that to some degree.

What frees us from the effects of malpractice is to stop malpracticing. There is no other way to be freed of the effects of malpractice than to stop malpracticing! Therefore the moment that I loose you and let you go, the moment that I say to you, "Neither do I judge thee; thy sins be forgiven thee," the moment I understand that God is your Father and that you are as pure as your Father—for you are of the same Life, Mind, and Substance—I have released you from malpractice and I have released myself from being a malpractitioner.

Since, now, I am not pouring out malpractice, none can come back to me, because my whole experience is made up of what I pour out. If I know the Truth, the Truth must make me free! If I know the Truth about you, that Truth makes me free because there is only One of us. There is only one Life, one Mind, one Soul. The Truth that I know about you is the Truth that makes me free.

The moment I stop malpracticing, I stop drawing malpractice unto myself. In other words: to be free, I must free you.

I can never be free while I am holding anyone in bondage. Never! The spiritual Law is that you must loose him and let him go. The spiritual Law is that you must forgive seventy times seven. The spiritual law is that you must behold God as the life of individual man. You must have the same discernment that Peter had when he said to the Master, "Thou art the Christ, the Son of the living God."

Look out at this world and say, "Thou art the Christ, the Son of the living God, and any evil that I see, hear, taste, touch, or smell is of the carnal mind. It has nothing to do with you. It has to do only with that Adamic belief in two powers." Now you can see that the measure of your outpouring is the measure of your incoming. It is just the same as the Law of supply. This is the same Law of supply at all other levels of life.

Unless you have had the experience of doing some healing work, you cannot comprehend what I am saying to you, at least not fully. If you once had the experience of doing healing work, this will open up to you in five minutes. Watch it do so!

An individual comes to a practitioner, more especially a practitioner of spiritual teaching, and asks for help. Now it may be that in them there is some sin, false appetite, criticism, judgment, or condemnation. There may be in them some manifestation of disease, but they have come now to the office of the spiritual practitioner, or to the consciousness. They may do it by telephone or mail, but in all events they have brought themselves to the consciousness of the practitioner. Watch now what happens in this practitioner's consciousness.

The request is made for help and the practitioner immediately lets thought go in the direction of God. "God is Spirit. God is the Spirit in man. God is Life, God is the Life of man. God is Soul, God is the Soul of man. God is the Source of all supply, God is the Supply of man. In fact, God constitutes man's being. Know ye not that ye are the Temple of God? Even your body is the Temple of God. God is perfect, and the offspring of God Is very God expressed! Just as a beam of sunlight is really the sun itself in an individual expression or form, the quality of a beam of sunlight is of the same quality as the sun itself, because it is the sun itself expressed. Therefore all that God is, man is. All that the Father hath, man hath, and nothing else! In fact, thou that seest me seest the Father that sent me. Thou that seest man seest the Creative Principle, because the Creative Principle—which is God—is expressed as man."

All of a sudden that person begins to feel a burden lift. First, perhaps, in the mind, and secondarily in the body. There is a release, or a relief. I can tell you what it is: the universal malpractice has been stopped. That malpractice that said you are a mortal, conceived in sin, brought forth in iniquity—a mortal who is sinning, a mortal who is guilty of omission or commission—is the universal malpractice that is upon every human being. You know it as well as I do; in your experience you have had over and over again this feeling of being unworthy.

I have read it so many times in my letters—"I am not worthy of God's Grace"—that I know it now by heart. I can recite it. But it is not true! No one is unworthy! God wouldn't let you live if you were unworthy! No one is unworthy, and no one has in himself any iniquity.

You remember the statement of Paul, "I know that I

am not perfect, but on the other hand, I know that I am not sinning; and yet I feel in me a sense of sin." So it is with every one of us! There is a universal sense of sin in all of us, because we know that in our humanhood we have never lived up to the full measure of our Christhood. No one ever has; no one ever can. This is not to claim that any *human being* is, or ever was, perfect. This is the Truth about *you*: *you* are perfect. *You* have never been a fallen man.

I am so happy to see that a hymn refers to "The Fabled Fall of Man." Of course there never was a fall of man! How could God's man fall? How could God let His man fall? All of this fall that you have heard about is the dream of mortal existence, which has come about by ascribing to yourself the sins of the carnal mind—which are not your sins at all. The moment the practitioner recognizes this, the universal malpractice is broken. Let me illustrate it in another way.

Let us suppose this is the flu season. Ten, twenty-five, a hundred, a thousand people come down with the flu. Do they all decide to sin and get the flu? Of course not! You know that the flu does not come because of any personal sins. It is a universal malpractice brought about by the belief in infection and contagion, and by the germ theory. It is a universal belief; it is a universal malpractice. That is all it is! So, whether one individual gets the flu or a thousand, it should not be difficult for you to meet it for the individuals and for your whole community if only you recognize it as a universal malpractice. Then drop it, because a universal malpractice is not authored by God, has no law of God to support it—and you do not have to fight it.

You see, in this message of The Infinite Way, our entire healing work is done by not taking up the sword. Our entire healing work is done by not using Truth over error, by not trying to have God heal a disease. Our entire healing work is done by a recognition of the Truth, the Truth being: that which is not of God has no law to sustain it; therefore you do not have to fight it—you only have to recognize it. The moment you recognize that an epidemic of any nature is but a universal malpractice, you do not have to fight it anymore. It has no power.

If God did not empower it, it has no power. The Master said to Pilate, *"Thou couldest have no power over me."* With all your temporal power, you could have no power over me. If the Master hadn't consented to crucifixion, I can assure you Pilate would never have been able to accomplish it. The Master had to consent to it and had to believe that it was going to be for the good of mankind.

When you know this Truth of true identity, think of yourself as being somewhere separate from mankind and looking out at them. Then realize that you are looking out at your Self, your divine Selfhood made manifest as a million or a billion people, and act that way toward them. Do not hold them in condemnation for their human thoughts, for that which they cannot help until they awaken to their true identity any more than you or I can help our human faults until we awaken to our true identity. We can try, psychologically, to be better—and we may succeed for a short time, until we repress our other side enough to make it come forth as an explosion, and then we will be worse than we were before.

I know this from experience. Before this first experience came to me, I knew all of my faults and I also knew how I would like to be without those faults, and I knew full well how I never succeeded in overcoming them. Then, when this experience came upon me, those faults disappeared of their own. Whatever the nature of this Christ was, they disappeared—the major ones, at least. I still have plenty of faults that my family could testify to, but at least they are not the major ones, and they are sufferable anyhow.

The point is, you cannot be any more loving than you are. You cannot be any more just, or merciful, or philanthropic; you cannot violate your own nature. However, in the moment that you begin to know the Truth, you break that human malpractice, anti-Christ, and you find that your nature changes. Your nature changes in proportion as you see my true nature. When you can look at me, not as a human being, not as a person with a past or a present or a future; when you look at me in the same way that I am looking at you and describing you—God is your Father, you are wholly spiritual in nature, perfection constitutes your being, infinity is the measure of your supply of Good, Truth is the Law of life unto you, immortality is your life span; as you begin to perceive this world in that way, you break the malpractice that has been upon you by breaking that malpractice of others.

Now, do you see the point that I am making? On the spiritual Path, it isn't this human life that is going to affect you, it is not people who are going to determine whether you are happy or unhappy, or prosperous or unprosperous; it is you who are going to determine it. You don't have to forsake your family. All of this takes place up in your consciousness. You may be living in an atmosphere of opposition to this Truth. If so, you don't ever have to voice it, you don't have to let anyone know you are thinking this Truth. Outwardly, you can conform: "Suffer it to be so now," or "Render unto Caesar the things that are Caesar's." You can say anything you want with your lips, but what is important is taking place in your consciousness.

I remember that years ago, when my life was entirely that of a practitioner in an office, occasionally some of us would come down with a cold in winter or some other minor ailment, and then it just seemed that the natural practice was to stay home and not let the patients know you were human. But this is ridiculous! Not only did I go to my office on those occasions, but one day when I was First Reader in the Christian Science church, I got up on the platform with two handkerchiefs in my hand. However, I was healed during that service. When I came off, I was told, "Oh, how wonderful that was; how wonderful!" I said, "If there are two hundred of you out there seeing me this way and giving me treatments, it has to work! If you were not giving me treatments, what *were* you doing out there?"

Then this cold is a malpractice, is it not? All I am suffering from is a malpractice—and one with God is a majority. (Two hundred ought to be two hundred majorities!) Therefore to know the Truth—that this is but a malpractice and not the Presence or Power of God—must free me. However, do you not see that in freeing me, it frees you too? Because a universal Truth, a Truth which you know, frees you. *"Ye shall know the Truth, and the Truth shall make you free,"* even if the Truth you are knowing is the Truth about me—any Truth that you know.

That is why we pray for others. We no longer have to pray for ourselves. You reach a place where you no longer think of praying for yourself or doing meditation or spiritual work for yourself. It just never enters your mind. Why? What is the difference between knowing the Truth about you and knowing the Truth about me? It is the same Truth, and we are the same Being, the same Selfhood. So knowing the Truth is all that is necessary, regardless of whether you are knowing it about the human race or about even the animal world or the bird world or the fish world.

It is for this reason that in my own work I am called upon very often by students and their families to help with their dogs or cats or birds. Sometimes someone is surprised that I am not too busy to do it, but what they do not understand is that it is just knowing the Truth. Now what difference does it make whether a bird benefits by it, or a cat, or a dog? In the end, I am the one who is really going to get the most benefit from it, because that knowing of the Truth is elevating me in consciousness above this picture.

The major Truth of all is: break the malpractice, break the anti-Christ that is holding man in bondage. Nothing else is holding him in bondage! Do not ever believe that man is held in bondage by people, do not ever believe that man is held in bondage by poverty or by disease. These are the *effects*! That is why it says in Scripture, "Lay the axe at the root of the tree"; do not start picking off branches!

The minute you heal a person of a headache, sure as fate, they will turn up with a footache, or a heartache. Heal them of a heartache, and the next thing you know it will be the liver, or the lungs, or the kidneys. It is nonsense to heal people of disease! Remove from them the malpractice of this universal belief in two powers. Remove from them this malpractice of the belief that they are human beings. That is what you have to do!

Then you find that they may have a half a dozen diseases and the whole half a dozen move out at one time, or they move out one at a time or two at a time. Watch them over the years. You will see how the dozen or so problems that we have when we come to this work gradually fade out, until we look back over a few years and realize, "None of those things have touched me for a long, long time."

You see: it is all up to you, and it is all up to me. It is the degree of the knowing of the Truth that I do that sets me free, even when it is the Truth about you. It, then, is breaking this malpractice!

CHAPTER 18

Christ of Being

Do NOT believe for a moment that if I hold someone in bondage, I myself am going to be free. That is utter nonsense! "As ye sow, so shall ye reap" is a law that cannot be broken. The only way to stop erroneous reaping is to stop erroneous sowing. Erroneous sowing only takes place "up here," in consciousness, in thought. It is determined by what I am willing to see "out there." Either I am willing to spiritually discern that you are the Christ, or I am going to judge by human appearances by saying, "Well, you are the child of Jones, Brown, or Smith." It is up to me! "Choose ye this day whom you will serve"— Truth or error, spiritual Truth or human knowledge.

If you choose spiritual Truth, you begin at any instant you like—and this is as good as any other—to take the attitude of sitting back, looking out at this world, and saying, "Thank God, I know thee now, who thou art. Thou art the very Christ of God, the son of God. Thank God, I know thee who thou art, the son of the Most High, offspring of God, heir of God, joint-heir with all of us to the spiritual Kingdom." "Son, thou art ever with God, and all that God hath is thine.'' This earth is the Lord's and the fullness thereof, and it belongs to each and every one of you!

Begin! Break the malpractice, break this anti-Christ, and begin to behold Christ. Know the Truth. At the same time, be sure that you do not put your head in the ground and say that there is no evil. Remember, all evil is an activity of the carnal mind, an activity of malpractice or anti-Christ; but because it is not of God, you don't have to fight it. Do not fight error! Do not try to overcome error; you can't, any more than you can overcome $2 \times 2 = 5$! Do not battle $2 \times 2 = 5$; just quietly know the Truth: $2 \times 2 = 4$. Don't argue about it, don't fight it, don't discuss it. There is nothing to discuss about 2×2; it is 4, and that is all there is to it.

Do not be interested in anyone's opinion. I can assure you there is nothing to discuss about Truth. The discussion of Truth is an utter waste of time, because there is nothing to be discussed. You are the Christ of being, and that is all there is to it! If anybody wants to discuss that with you, let them go home and discuss it with themselves. Do not waste time.

The Truth is that all evil is impersonal, it is a universal belief in two powers. It is a universal malpractice or anti-Christ. There is no use discussing that. That is Truth. Discussing it will not change it; it may make you doubt it in the end. However, holding to it, abiding in it, and proving it: this is the whole story.

That is why, when this Truth is presented to you, you should be very careful that you do not present it to anyone else. Be very careful that you keep it locked up inside of you as a very sacred secret until you can demonstrate it. If you go around talking about it, discussing it, somebody is going to call your bluff and say, ''Prove it!'' Then you will have to be like the man who said, "Oh, no! I teach the Truth, but I do not heal." Now you know that can't be—no more than an airplane instructor can instruct if he can't pilot. At least you would not want him to instruct you if you felt he couldn't pilot.

Truth is not subject to discussion. There are certain laws of Truth that have been laid down by the mystics who have been God-inspired or God-endowed. When you hear or read these Truths, either you know that it is Truth or you are not ready for it. If you are not ready for it, keep on searching. However, if you do feel the rightness of what you hear or what you read, keep it very sacred and very secret. Lock it up inside of yourself and practice it— because it is all taking place "up here" in your consciousness. Then, when you begin to witness the fruitage of it and someone comes to you and says, "What is Truth?" you can begin to explain what you yourself have learned and are demonstrating. However, do not permit them to discuss it with you. Do not do that. I can assure you, they will prove to you that you are all wrong.

There was a reason why the Master taught that you should not pray to be seen of man. When you pray, retire into the inner sanctuary of your own being and do your praying in there, and let the evidence of your praying be outwardly manifested. *The Father that seeth in secret, rewardeth thee openly.* If you do all of your treating in secret, all of your praying in secret, the results will appear outwardly. Then, when you are called upon to explain or teach, you can.

However, when you do, be so well prepared within yourself, be so convinced, that you do not ever permit anyone to discuss it with you. Never! Not in all my years in this work have I ever permitted anyone to discuss Truth with me. I state it and there it has to be. Take it or leave it; but do not discuss it with me, do not argue it with me. I am not interested. This is it—the way it has been revealed; and I can demonstrate it. But that is the end of it!

Are we still under the law or are we under Grace? We almost can answer that ourselves if we stop to think. Can you, for a moment, conceive of praying in some way that you will not be asking for anything, expecting anything, desiring anything? Could you possibly think, in your mind, of a prayer that would have in it no element at all of wanting to benefit from the prayer?

This sounds very gentle as I give it to you, but I can assure you that when you think it over, it could make you very angry. If you ever seriously undertake to pray, pray without ceasing—but pray prayers that have in them no desire, no expectancy, no wish, for the getting of anything, receiving or attaining of anything. You will find that before you can successfully attain to that degree of spiritual praying, you will nearly tear yourself to pieces.

It becomes very difficult to take the attitude of, "God, I do not want anything. I do not need anything, I am not coming to You for anything. I am releasing You. You have no responsibility to me whatsoever. There is nothing that I need, there is nothing You have that I want."

Then think of all the different things that come up in your life that it was believed, for centuries, God could give you. Then you will see what a terrible tearing apart of ourselves it is, once we begin to live this other life.

There is a statement in our textbook, *The Infinite Way*, that, if it were understood, would make a lot of enemies for me. My good fortune is that only my friends have understood it. I keep praying that it will always be that way—because this statement says, "That which I am seeking, *I Am*."

Now, what does this do to your sense of prayer? "That

which I am seeking": what am I seeking? Truth? *I AM* the Truth. Am I seeking God? *I Am* God. Am I seeking supply? *I Am* the bread, the meat, the wine, and the water. Am I seeking health? *I Am* the Resurrection and the Life.

That one sentence in the book could change a person's entire life. It would, if it were understood, and if we developed the capacity to live it so that at any moment when the thought came to mind that "I need, I want, I desire, I wish I had"—or when our thought reached out to God for anything—this sentence would come back to us: "That which I am seeking, I am." Then you would also find your muscles tensing and your face getting rigid, because now you would have to stand pat on "I cannot desire anything, I cannot want anything, I cannot even go to God for anything. I have to abide in this Truth: That which I am seeking, *I Am. I Am* the Way and the Truth. The Kingdom of God is neither lo, here, nor lo, there. *I Am!*" Do you see what happens?

If you are abiding under the Truth that "I and my Father are One," you are under Grace, because you are living by such promises as "Son, thou art ever with me, all that *I* have is thine." Now just take that scriptural promise, "All that *I* have is thine": it all comes back to *I*—all that *I* have! Now *I*, the Father, and I, the son, are One, according to Scripture and according to revealed mystical Truth. I and my Father are One.

I, the Father, and I, the son, Am One. Therefore, what has *I*, the Father, that I, the son, hasn't got if *I*, the Father, and I, the son, are One? The point is now to live in that constant remembrance. All that the Father hath is mine, for *I*, the Father, and I, the son, Is One. That keeps you from reaching out to God; and of course, it breaks all attachment to this world.

It also keeps you from reaching out to "man, whose

breath is in his nostrils." You no longer expect justice from man, or love, or benevolence, or anything else. You know, now, that all that I receive, I am to receive from the Father—and yet not receive: because all that is embodied in the Father is embodied in the son. Prayer has to be that constant recognition, "Thank you, Father, *I Am*." It is not "I need," not "I want," not "I shall be, or should be," or even "I deserve to be," but *I Am*!

Now think of a prisoner saying, "I am free." That has to be the attitude, since I and my Father are One, and all that the Father hath is mine. The freedom of the Christ is the freedom of my individual being. Despite all appearances, we have to live and move in that consciousness. Supposing, that instead of the prison of that nature, we are imprisoned in an appetite, a sin, a disease. In spite of the appearance, we know now that there is no use praying to God to release us from our diseases, because God is no more going to do it for us than for all those people in the hospitals.

There has to be a different Truth than praying to God for something, and here it is: the spiritual freedom of the Father Is the spiritual freedom of the son. Where the Spirit of the Lord is, there Is liberty. Since *I*, the Father, and I, the son, are One, then the Spirit of the Lord Is where *I Am*. Here, where I Am, God Is. The place whereon I stand Is holy ground because I and the Father are One! You see, you are now abiding in Truth.

Well, as you abide in truth, you will find that the prison bars, whether they are iron bars or disease bars or sin bars, begin to break. Sometimes miracles happen in a flash, and sometimes it takes days, weeks, and months for these miracles to dissolve the particular fetters that bind us. However, the point is that there must be a constant living, moving, and having your being in the Truth that *I Am* the Truth. Not that there is a Truth that will free me, not that there is a God that will heal me, but that I and my Father are One, and all that the Father hath is mine. The place whereon I stand is holy ground because the Spirit of the Lord God is here where *I Am*. The Kingdom of God is neither lo here, nor lo there. It Is within me.

Then why am I praying for anything when I have Omniscience within me, the All-knowing? Why am I praying for anything if I have Omnipotence within me, the All-power? Why am I praying to a God when I have Omnipresence within me? In other words, God is no further from me than my own breathing. Since God is the All-knowing, I do not have to pray to God for anything. I have to abide in the Truth of my Oneness with God.

Now you see, nothing enters your experience except through your consciousness—nothing! Whatever it is that you are to experience in your life, you must experience through your own consciousness. There is no outside God, there is no outside devil, there are no outside laws. Whatever it is that is operating in you is operating through and in your own consciousness, and it is one of two things.

You have either a consciousness of Truth or a consciousness of ignorance of Truth. If you are ignorant of Truth, you are not made free. If you know the Truth, the Truth will make you free. Therefore it is knowing, or consciousness. You must consciously know the Truth! Do not sit around waiting for some mysterious God to do something for you because you are charitable, or kind, or moral. It will not work! It is your abiding in the Truth, your abiding in the Word, letting the Word abide in you. It is your abiding in God and letting God abide in you. You are the one who is doing it.

The moment you stop preying on God, you will find that you have discovered the secret of answered prayer.

The moment you are no longer the parasite seeking to draw something from God, instead living in the realization of "That which I am seeking, *I am*" since *I*, the Father, and I, the son, are One: by consciously knowing this Truth, I am abiding in the consciousness of Truth. I am abiding in the Word, and the Word is abiding in me. I have to hold to that while ignoring the appearances that would testify to my present lacks and limitations. We can't deny that we have lacks and limitations at the moment; they're too apparent. But we can begin to ignore them while we abide in the Truth. Let the Truth dissolve them, dissipate them.

To live under Grace, then, means to give up the use of the law. Giving up the use of the law is giving up the use of a lot of beliefs, too. There was a time when we used to believe that because we were in spiritual work, God would see that we had ample supply. Then we found out that God did not much care whether we were in spiritual work or not. The supply just was not there.

As a matter of fact, to God, there is no such thing as spiritual work. There is no one needing supply, therefore, there is no function on the part of God to supply. You must move out from the belief that because you were born, God owes you a living, or God owes you supply—or because you are a good wife or a good husband or a good housewife or a good parent or a good employee or a good employer, that you deserve supply. This is all in the realm of fiction. Nobody deserves supply. Everybody has infinite supply who recognizes their relationship to God. This is the only spiritual source of supply.

Humanly, there are thousands of ways of getting money and properties and securities. Spiritually, there is only one way. It is not by earning it or deserving it. It is not by being worthy of it. It is not by giving God 10 percent so that you get back 90 percent. It is not sacrificing to God. It is not spending so many hours a day in prayer to God. There is only one way to enjoy the infinite abundance of God, and that is through knowing the Truth. The Truth you have to know is your relationship to God.

I and the Father are One. *I*, the Father, and I, the son, are One. The Father is always saying, *"Son, all that I have is thine."* As long as I keep looking to *I*, I will be abundantly supplied.

Now, what does this do to human nature? We have been taught for centuries that a husband owes his wife supply, and the wife really loves to believe it. It is so comforting to know this: "He owes it to me." In a state like California he had better give it, too! If you come under the law there, you will find no mercy!

What does it take to release your husband from the obligation to support you? What kind of an effort do you think that it really takes inside of yourself to say, "I free you, I loose you. I accept from you whatever out of love you give, and I accept that as the love of God; but I release you from human responsibility or legal responsibility, because I am accepting my divine relationship to God. I am declaring that I and my Father are One, and my Father has many infinite ways of bringing unto me that which is my own." Now, you will find that is not easy. We have centuries behind us of the belief that someone else is responsible for our women.

Do not think for a moment that this makes it easy for the men. They have something equally serious that is holding them in bondage. They believe that their supply is from their business, their profession, their inheritance, or their investments. Of course, in this modern day, what would the world do without its Social Security and old age? I do not know.

What do you think that it really takes for a man to go within and say, "I will continue to work and to love my work, but I release you from the strain of believing that my supply is dependent on you. I have my intimate relationship with my Source. I have my personal relationship with my Father. I and the Father are One"?

For example, think of the salesman releasing his customers. "I look not to you for my sales. I sell as part of my business activity; but, thank God, you have no control over my supply. I and my Father are One. My supply is mine in relationship to my conscious awareness."

Do you see how you are bringing yourself out from under the law of human belief, of human relationships, of human channels of supply, and bringing yourself back under Grace? No one can permanently bring you under Grace but yourself. Every time a practitioner brings about a healing for you—physical, mental, moral, or financial—they have released you from whatever law was operating and brought you under Grace. That is all there is to spiritual healing; it is releasing the patient from under the law.

Remember, under the law there are certain germs that give you a cold and certain germs that give you polio, certain germs that give you this, that, or the other thing. This is a law, and if you are very sensible, you will not tell a doctor that it is *not* a law. It *is* the law; but every time you turn to a spiritual healer, the healer has to remove you from under this law and bring you under Grace to where that law of infection or contagion—that law of food or of climate—is not operating.

You see, there is no such thing as anyone separating you permanently from being under the law or from being under all of the law. It is something you do yourself. Your practitioner does it for you in that acute condition for which you turn for help. However, if a practitioner could do it for you permanently and completely, he would be too busy for you. The millionaires would hire him up right away and he would have no time left for you. You must see that this is something money will not buy! You can't even hire a practitioner or teacher by the month, year, or life. It will not work! You have to move from being under the law to being under Grace.

Surely in any emergency the practitioner who knows the Truth can bring you out from under the law and place you under Grace in that particular situation, and the next one and the next one. Remember, though, that it has been a universal experience that after a few years, it does not work any more. In other words, sooner or later students must begin to bring themselves out consciously from under the law and bring themselves under Grace. They must at some time or other release themselves from old-fashioned prayers or metaphysical prayers that seek to gain something, get something, receive something, achieve something—even from God.

Release God and let Him go! Say outright, "You owe me nothing and I seek nothing from You or of You, for You have already imparted Yourself to me, and all that Thou hast is mine." You begin to live under that divine Grace, and then you find you are under the law less and less. Less and less you are under the law of weather, climate, and food. Less and less you are under the law of infection and contagion. Less and less you are under the law of age and calendars. And more and more you move into a life by Grace. It is a gradual process.

It is true that when we come to a culmination point, a transitional point, something happens, and in the twinkling of an eye we are completely under Grace. At a certain period of our experience, the fetters fall away, the law falls away, the past falls away, and we are under Grace.

Actually, we have brought ourselves there through the years of seeking God, seeking Truth, seeking Realization.

Because of our years of study and of meditation, we gradually slough off traits of humanhood and thus prepare ourselves for a certain moment. It is like that of Saul of Tarsus, who for many years had studied under the greatest masters and for years had devoted himself heart and soul to the Temple and to his concept of God. Then in one blinding flash he is free; he realizes the Christ; and Saul of Tarsus is "dead" and Paul is alive. So we have a man now saying, "I can do all things through Christ. I live, yet not I; Christ liveth my life."

This is what happens on the spiritual Path. Day by day we break some fetter of human experience and we drop some phase of humanness. We make that transition to where our prayer now is a benediction to the world, to where we are no longer praying that we receive anything but we are praying, "Father, forgive our enemies, they know not what they do. Father, forgive those who have despitefully used me, they know not what they do. Father, forgive all those who are not in Thy Grace and bring them under Thy Grace."

In other words, we have made an about-face and we are no longer sitting at the feet of the Master. We now *are* the Master, and we are healing the multitudes, freeing the multitudes, and feeding and forgiving the multitudes. We are now the Christ Consciousness, and we seek nothing for ourselves, because we know that "all that the Father hath is already mine." Now our whole life is pouring forth God's Grace to this world, but not in the form of throwing our pearls before swine to be trampled on. We do it silently and secretly. Our praying is done in secret!

CHAPTER 19

When Christ Has Entered In

OUR PRAYING is done in secret. *The Father that seeth in secret will reward thee openly."* Therefore we do not go around blessing our fellow-man so that he can see us do it or know that we are doing it. It has to be a secret within ourself, known only to ourself and to the Father within.

As someone on the outer plane is led to us and asks questions, or seeks, we can begin to share with them. If we are wise, we will do it as the Master said. We will give milk to the babes and meat to the adults. We will begin to pour out, very gently, this milk of the Word, until we see that those who have come to us are ready for more and more Truth. Then, ultimately, we will pour it all out and give it all to them.

However, this life of prayer is not the life of prayer that is "going to God to get blessings." It is the life of prayer that fits us to be a blessing so that we come out from sitting at the feet of the Master forever. We become the master who walks up and down the earth, silently, secretly saying, "Neither do I judge thee. Neither do I condemn

thee. Thy sins be forgiven thee. Thou art the Temple of
God and God Is in His holy Temple. The Peace of God
Is with you. The Presence of God Is with you. The Omniscience of God Is with you. The place whereon thou
standest Is holy ground.''

You are the master now, you are the Christ consciousness now. No longer are you a selfhood apart from God,
seeking, needing, desiring. Now you are the Way, the
Life, and the Truth—and you can only be that as long as
you keep it a secret. You can only be that as long as you
make it a secret relationship between you and your Father,
until somebody evolves to the extent where you can reveal
this to them.

Here we take the reverse angle of prayer, not using it
for our benefit, or for our patients' or students' benefit.
We have adopted prayer as a way of life in the sense of
the "outgivingness" of life, not the "incomingness." This
is prayer as a way of life lived by the Master, the way of
life lived as Christ consciousness.

That has always been your goal. You have always
prayed, "Give me Christ consciousness"; you have always
prayed, "O that I might receive the Christ!" You have always prayed; however, this is *attaining* it! This is accepting
it! But you can only accept it by a reversal; not by sitting
at the feet of the Master. You can only accept it by saying, "I and the Father are One, and all of God's Grace
that flows to me will flow out from me, through me, to
this world." This is the only way you can really pray for
the world.

You cannot pray that peace come on earth, and I will
tell you why. If peace came on earth tomorrow, there
would be war the day after. There would have to be: because man's consciousness is not changed! How are you
going to have peace on earth while there is war in con-

sciousness? Do you not see that? All the peace treaties in the world would be of no avail unless men and women were ready for peace.

It is the same way when we pray for prosperity. After we get it, do we not waste it? Think of the amount of it that is thrown away—and then you would say, "Well, we had it but we did not know enough to hold on to it." There is no use praying for prosperity until you have the consciousness to know what to do with it when you have it. Gain the consciousness of it first, and then the rest will be added.

So it is that you have prayed for the Christ to enter your soul. As a matter of fact, the title of my book *The World Is New* is based on the quotation that is in the chapel at Stanford University, selected by Mrs. Stanford herself: "The world is new to every soul when Christ has entered in." Now, are you going to sit around forever waiting for Christ to enter in? It will not happen!

We have been preparing human consciousness to receive the Christ. Consciousness has been prepared to accept the Truth that "I and the Christ are One." Now is the time to accept it. Now is the time to move from being an individual who continues to pray to God for things to being the individual who surrenders that, who surrenders even the right to pray in that sense, and understands: "Now I and the Father are One. We have united consciously. We have always been One; but now *consciously* I and the Father are One, and all that the Father hath Is mine. Therefore, my life, now, is one of bestowal, one of benediction, one of sharing."

Then you are sitting back and looking out there, not as a suppliant at the feet of the Master, but instead sitting to the right of the Master as a co-worker with the Master, a disciple of the Master, an apostle of the Master, engaged in the same activity: sharing God's Grace with humanity. The best way to do it is to pray, " 'Thy sins be forgiven thee.' Father, open their eyes.''

Individual peace will come into your life when you are ready for it, and not before. When you stop taking up the sword of criticism, judgment, condemnation, malpractice, the sword will not be taken up against you. In that moment when you decide to live under Grace, under love, judging no man: that is the moment when peace will come into your individual experience.

No matter how many bombs fly, no matter how many thousands fall at your left or at your right, it will not come nigh thy dwelling place. You will also be the means of saving many others who are embodied in your consciousness. Peace will come to you when peace is established within you, when you establish peace with your fellow-man.

Prosperity—that is, spiritual prosperity—will come to you when you are fit to receive it by your giving of your first fruits to God, by your giving of your conscious awareness to mankind. When you become either the master, or the disciple, or the apostle, that becomes the instrument through which God's Grace flows to mankind. Peace and prosperity will then come into your experience, and you will also hasten the day when it will come to mankind. Mankind is still going to hold to its arrogant nature until there are enough Christ apostles and disciples walking the earth, forgiving and praying for the enemy, to soften them up.

Never believe that if they scrap all the armies, navies, and air forces, this will bring an era of peace on earth; because it will not! I have twice witnessed navies scrapped, I have several times seen peace treaties signed, and it does not mean a thing. They are all scraps of paper, because behind them there is not the intent to keep them. In other words, there is not yet the mellowness of love in human consciousness.

Once that mellowness comes into human consciousness, we will not need treaties any more than we need one with Canada. We do not have any peace treaties with Canada, nor do we have any armies and navies at the Canadian border, because there has entered on that side of the border and this side of the border a consciousness of peace. Yes, there will be troubles between Canada and the United States at times; always in human relationships there arise disturbing elements. But this is not war. It cannot eventuate in war, because peace is already established in the consciousness of North Americans, and there will not be war.

So it is you will discover that war cannot enter your life if it has been ruled out of your consciousness. But it cannot be ruled out of your consciousness while you are living on the human plane, which is under the law. It can only be ruled out of your consciousness if you will accept yourself as Christ, or as the disciple or apostle of Christ, and say, "I have removed myself from this side to that side: I am now sitting at that place where my life is a forgiveness, a benediction, a blessing; and no evil can come nigh me, because I am not seeking anything, I am not even seeking good. As long as I am not seeking, I am not going to receive, I will always Be." This is our real nature: Being! I and the Father are One in Being, in Essence. I and the Father are Being life, we are Being eternal life. *I Am* immortal life!

When do you move from that seat at the feet of the Master that says, "Give me life"? When do you move to the seat beside the Master and say, "Thou hast given me life eternal. I am life eternal." When do we move from asking the Master to be fed, to saying, "Thou hast fed me

Truth, and now I know: all that God Is, I am; all that the Father hath Is mine."

We can bring about a transition in consciousness if we will start a battle with ourselves. That battle will start the very moment that we realize that we have had the privilege taken away from us of going to God for something—or to man. We have had to sit still and say, "No." Even out in the middle of the Pacific Ocean in a rubber boat: "All that God Is, I am, and all that the Father hath Is mine."

Even in the midst of prison, or a prison of sin, or a prison of disease, I am going to close my eyes to the appearance and say, "No more begging, no more pleading, no more looking out," now realizing, "Thank you, Father. All that God Is, I am. That which I am seeking, I Am. All that the Father hath Is mine. Here, where I am, Is holy ground, for here the Spirit of the Lord Is; and where the Spirit of the Lord Is, there Is liberty."

These lessons have involved a movement in consciousness, a transition in consciousness, from sitting at the feet of the Master to sitting up at the table with the Master. "I have received from the Master. From Truth I have received life eternal. I have received divine Grace. I have received the assurance of my Oneness with God. Now it is my turn to share, to bless, to pray."

In praying for the world, there is one mode and means of prayer that will do more to break the evils of the human mind than anything else: realize that God, Spirit, is Omnipotence, and therefore the mind of man is not power, the will of man is not power, the way of man is not power. All power is in God, Spirit, and therefore there is no power in the carnal mind, or mortal mind, or human mind, whichever you call it. All power Is in God.

Remember, Christ is not a temporal power that goes out and destroys enemies. Christ is not a power that can go out and help you get a better bargain at someone else's expense. Christ is the gentle Presence that establishes peace in the heart, mind, and souls of men. Look upon Christ as the gentle Influence that cements men in their spiritual relationship. Do not look on God or Christ as a temporal power that you can invoke to go out and do something. However, understand that the carnal mind of man is not power and that the gentle influence of the Christ Is the dissolving of all that is adamant in human consciousness.

To pray for the world means to look out and almost see this globe of the universe in front of you and feel your hands, or your love, going out around that globe, saying, "Father, forgive them; they know not what they do." "I pray that thy sins be forgiven thee. I pray that Christ dwell in thy heart. I pray that no penalties ever be inflicted upon you for the past. I pray that you know spiritual Freedom, spiritual Justice, spiritual Life, and spiritual Law." Hold that globe this way, in a whole armful of love, understanding, and forgiveness. Allow no thought of victory to enter your mind; no victory over man, no victory over ideologies, no victory over countries. Not victories; Peace!

There never can be Peace when there are victories, because with every victory there is a loss, and the loser must always think about the next gain. Never think of victories; think of Peace. "My Peace give I unto you." Keep that globe in your arms. "My Peace give I unto you, not as the world giveth." My Peace, spiritual Peace, the Peace that brings with it forgiveness, comfort. "My Comfort give I unto you—spiritual Comfort."

Remember, you have moved. You are not sitting at the feet of the Master; you are sitting on the platform *with* the Master. Therefore you have the equal right as a disciple and apostle to place your arms around the globe and say, "My Peace give I unto you, not as the world giveth. My Grace is thy sufficiency." It is not charity, not benevolence, not somebody's generous pocketbook: "My Grace is thy sufficiency." You are speaking out as a disciple of the Master.

The most difficult situation arises with yourself in the early months when you have to consciously resist the temptation to want something and desire something as if you were out there at the feet of the Master. You have to consciously remember that you gave up that seat to those who are not yet aware. Now your seat is on the platform. You are sitting up there, a co-worker with the Christ of God. Your function is no longer to receive but to bestow. Your function is not to get but to give. Your question that you must ask yourself every morning is, "What have I in the house?" Then throughout the day, as the opportunity comes to bestow the Bread of life, the Meat, the Wine, the Water, the Life, the Resurrection, remember that this is the Path you have embarked upon.

Again, it is like degrees. The spiritual life is lived in degrees like a fraternal order: first degree, second degree, all the way up to the thirty-third degree. You have voluntarily surrendered your rights as a first degree, or a second degree, and you have claimed for yourself the title of the third degree. You have claimed for yourself discipleship with the Master. Therefore you cannot any more go back to being the person in the first and the second degrees. Now, you must be the one who shares the light of the third degree with those coming up through the first and second degrees.

Each day you have to remember, "What have I in the house?—from my standpoint now, of a disciple, an apostle." You will find you are living your life in a different dimension. Certainly you will find that you are living under Grace, because now, like the disciples, you can go out without purse or scrip and find that your needs will be met, without taking thought.

Are we still under the law or are we under Grace? That depends on which side of the table you are sitting on. It depends on whether you are looking out at people, remembering what they owe you and seeing to it that you get it, or whether you have come to realize your relationship with God, understanding yourself to be the bestower, the giver, the sharer of His Glory.

You are not giving anything of yourself. You will not be one penny poorer after you give away a thousand dollars, because it is not yours that you are giving. That, too, determines whether you are under the law or under Grace. Do you believe that your personal possessions are yours, or do you see that the earth is the Lord's and the fullness thereof, and that God is just expressing them through you?

That makes us transfer agents. We are not givers of our own. We are not givers of ourself. We are merely transfer agents. *"The earth is the Lord's and the fullness thereof. All that I have is thine."* Keep your eyes on that word *"I."* *All that I have is thine*—I and the Father being One. I have allness to give, to share, to bestow. So it is that we move up from the feet of the Master to a place beside Him at the table!